STANDING FIRM IN A DECEPTIVE WORLD

DR. SADAF TAJ

ZORBA BOOKS

ZORBA BOOKS

Published by Zorba Books, April 2026
Website: www.zorbabooks.com
Email: info@zorbabooks.com
Author Name: Dr. Sadaf Taj

Title: Standing Firm in a Deceptive World

Printbook ISBN: 978-93-5896-390-8
Ebook ISBN: 978-93-5896-769-2

Zorba Books Pvt. Ltd. (opc)
Sushant Arcade,
Next to Courtyard Marriot,
Sushant Lok 1, Gurgaon - 122009, India

Printed in India

In the Name of Allah, the Most Merciful, the Most Compassionate

فَإِنَّ مَعَ الْعُسْرِ يُسْرًا

"For indeed, with hardship [will be] ease." (Quran 94:5)

Contents

Acknowledgement

First and foremost, I offer my deepest gratitude to Almighty God, whose guidance and grace carried me through every chapter of this journey. This book is a reflection of faith, hope, and divine timing.

Many of these stories unfolded in moments of stillness. Some chapters took shape in quiet mornings, others in whispered prayers and reflective pauses—those rare moments when the noise of the world seemed to fade and the heart could listen more clearly.

To my children, thank you for honoring the quiet spaces I needed to write. Your patience and understanding made this journey possible. I extend my heartfelt gratitude to my husband, **Kashif Baig**, for taking time out of his busy schedule to proofread my work.

I am also deeply thankful to my mother, family, and friends. Your constant encouragement, warmth, and presence allowed this book to grow naturally and without haste.

Above all, I hope these stories encourage readers to pause, breathe, and reconnect with their inner faith and wisdom.

Preface

This book began with a simple thought—an attempt to reflect on the relationship between a believer and the Creator in the quiet moments of everyday life. What started as a small idea slowly grew into a collection of stories that explore how faith accompanies us through the ordinary and the extraordinary alike.

The pages that follow are not tales of perfect people. They are stories of ordinary individuals from different walks of life—people who face doubts, hardships, temptations, and difficult choices. Like all of us, they struggle to understand the world around them. Yet through their journeys, one truth slowly reveals itself: when a heart turns sincerely towards God, guidance often appears in ways we never expected.

These stories were written with the hope of inviting readers to pause and reflect on the deeper meaning behind the events of daily life. Sometimes faith is strengthened in moments of ease, and sometimes it is rediscovered in moments of confusion or trial. In either case, the journey of the human heart toward its Creator remains one of the most profound experiences in life.

It is my humble hope that these stories will resonate with readers and inspire moments of reflection. If even one story encourages someone to look at life with renewed faith, patience, or gratitude, then this effort will have been worthwhile.

Thank you for taking the time to read these pages and for joining me on this journey of reflection and faith.

– Sadaf Taj

Chapter 1

Hamza – A Journey From Confusion to Clarity

Hamza was the kind of child who naturally drew people toward him. Allah had blessed him with a face that seemed to glow with innocence and a smile that softened even the hardest expressions. His laughter filled rooms, and his presence often brightened gatherings without him even realizing it. Relatives adored him, neighbors spoke fondly of him, and visitors were always charmed by the way he greeted them—respectfully, warmly, and with a sweetness that felt genuine rather than rehearsed.

Being the youngest among his siblings meant that Hamza grew up surrounded by an extra layer of affection. His brothers and sisters hovered around him with protective pride, often indulging his smallest wishes. His childhood unfolded in a home filled with laughter, security, and the quiet reassurance that he was deeply loved.

Naturally, such affection sometimes made Hamza a little stubborn. When things did not go his way, he could insist on his point with surprising determination. Yet even his stubbornness carried a certain innocence that made it difficult for anyone to remain angry with him for long.

But Hamza possessed something more than charm.

He possessed curiosity.

Questions seemed to live permanently in his mind. He watched everything carefully—the way people spoke, the way situations unfolded, the way adults reacted to the world around them. Whenever something puzzled him, he asked about it without hesitation. To Hamza, asking questions was simply part of understanding life.

One afternoon, while playing inside the house, he noticed something unusual.

His mother was sitting quietly on her prayer mat. Her head was lowered, and her shoulders trembled slightly. As Hamza walked closer, he saw tears rolling slowly down her cheeks.

The sight startled him.

For a child, a mother's tears are deeply unsettling. A mother's smile is comfort; her sadness feels like the world losing its balance.

Concerned, Hamza rushed to her side.

"Ammi," he asked softly, tugging at her sleeve, "why are you crying?"

His mother looked up, surprised. Seeing the worry in her little son's eyes, she immediately pulled him close and wrapped her arms around him. For a moment she held him tightly, as though drawing strength from his innocent presence.

Then she smiled gently through her tears.

"My dear child," she said softly, "these are not tears of sadness."

Hamza looked at her with confusion.

"I am crying before my Lord," she continued, stroking his hair, "thanking Him for blessing me with such a wonderful Hamza. And I am praying for your success, and for the success of your brothers and sisters."

Hamza did not fully understand the depth of her words, but something about that moment settled quietly into his heart.

The image of his mother crying in prayer stayed with him long afterward. It was his first glimpse into a world that children rarely see—the silent conversations between a believer and their Creator.

From that day onward, the idea of prayer felt different to him.

Surrounded by affection and guided by his parents' care, Hamza's early years blossomed peacefully. His childhood was filled with warmth, curiosity, and the comfort of belonging.

By the age of seven, he already knew many stories about the prophets. His mother would often tell him about their lives—their patience, their struggles, and their unwavering faith in Allah even during the most difficult times.

Yet these stories stirred questions in Hamza's mind.

"If Allah has so much power," he once asked thoughtfully, "why did the prophets have to suffer so much?"

And sometimes he would add another question, one that puzzled him even more.

"And why haven't we ever seen Allah?"

His mother never dismissed his curiosity. With patience and wisdom, she answered in ways that his young mind could understand—offering gentle explanations without overwhelming him with complexities.

These conversations quietly planted seeds within Hamza's heart. Even as a child, he began to think deeply about faith, life, and the unseen realities that lay beyond human understanding.

As the years passed, those questions did not fade. Instead, they grew stronger.

By the time Hamza turned fourteen, his mind often wandered toward thoughts about existence, truth, and the trials faced by people who stood firmly for what they believed in.

Around that time, his elder sister got married.

Her departure left the house feeling strangely different. Some days it felt quieter, as though a familiar melody had suddenly disappeared. Yet whenever she returned to visit, bringing laughter and warmth back into the home, the house seemed alive again.

Years moved quickly.

By the time Hamza turned eighteen, his sister had become the mother of two beautiful children. Hamza adored his niece and nephew completely. He played with them endlessly, fulfilled their little wishes, and spoiled them with affection whenever he could.

One day, however, an incident occurred that left a lasting impression on him.

His four-year-old nephew had accidentally broken an expensive vase while playing. The sharp sound of shattering glass echoed through the room.

Startled and frustrated, Hamza's sister scolded the child harshly.

The boy immediately burst into tears.

Hamza felt anger rise within him.

"How can you scold such a small child like that?" he protested, clearly upset. To him, the sight of the crying child felt unbearable.

But a few moments later, he noticed something unexpected.

His sister's anger quickly faded. Regret appeared on her face. She picked up the child, wiped away his tears, and began feeding him gently, showering both children with affection—as though trying to erase the harshness of her earlier reaction.

Hamza watched quietly.

In that moment, he understood something he had never fully realized before. A mother's heart carried many emotions at once—anger, love, regret, and tenderness—all woven together in ways that outsiders rarely understood.

That day, Hamza gained his first glimpse into the complexity of motherhood.

A few months later, another important moment arrived in his life.

Hamza was preparing to move to another city to pursue higher studies.

For his parents, this decision brought both pride and anxiety. The world outside their home felt very different from the protected environment in which Hamza had grown up. Society was changing rapidly, exposing young people to influences that many families found troubling.

Discussions about sexuality, increasing exposure to drugs and alcohol, and shifting social values worried them deeply. Like many Muslim parents, they wondered how their son would navigate such an environment while holding on to his faith.

As the day of his departure approached, Hamza's mother found herself overwhelmed with emotion. Often she wept quietly in prayer, asking Allah to protect her son wherever he went.

His father tried to comfort her.

"Leave everything to Allah," he said gently. "Pray sincerely for him. A parent's prayer is the strongest protection."

When the day finally arrived, Hamza left for the new city with mixed emotions. Part of him felt excited about the new chapter ahead. Another part felt the heaviness of leaving the warmth of home.

He promised himself that he would remain focused on his studies and stay true to the values he had been raised with.

Yet when he arrived at the university, he quickly noticed that the environment was very different from what he had known.

Many students seemed detached from deeper purpose. Their lives revolved around parties, entertainment, and fleeting pleasures. Discussions about ethics or faith rarely appeared in their conversations.

At times, Hamza felt like an outsider among them.

But he also saw this experience as a test—an opportunity to prove his strength and character.

Within his extended circle of friends were individuals who openly identified as gay or lesbian. In the university environment, this was considered normal and widely accepted.

Gradually, Hamza began absorbing the influence of this new social atmosphere.

He started thinking that if two people genuinely loved each other and found happiness together, perhaps there was no reason for society to object. The question that troubled him most was why Islam appeared so strict on this matter.

Why, he wondered, was homosexuality considered sinful or immoral?

The questions that had once been simple childhood curiosities were now returning with greater intensity.

And Hamza had only just begun his journey of searching for answers.

Hamza's homosexual friends did not resemble the image he had grown up hearing about.

They were not cruel, reckless, or immoral people. In fact, many of them stood firmly against injustice. They were compassionate, often quick to help others, and deeply sensitive to the suffering around them. Some volunteered for social causes, others supported friends during difficult times with remarkable loyalty.

The more Hamza interacted with them, the more confused he became.

Their character did not match the negative stereotypes he had always heard. Instead, he saw kindness, empathy, and sincerity—qualities that any faith would praise.

Slowly, this contrast began to reshape his perception of things he had once accepted without question.

The doubts that had first appeared in childhood now returned with greater intensity. Why worship a God who could not be seen? Why follow divine commandments whose wisdom was not always immediately clear? Were these rules truly meant for all times, or were they bound to another era?

Yet Hamza was not someone who rejected ideas carelessly.

One of his strongest traits was his determination to seek understanding. When questions troubled him, he did not brush them aside. Instead, he pursued answers with patience and seriousness. He read books on religion and philosophy, listened to debates between scholars, and even explored the teachings of other faiths in the hope of gaining clarity.

His search was not fueled by arrogance, but by sincerity.

He did not want to abandon faith—he wanted to understand it.

Living away from his family meant that Hamza was now surrounded by an environment far more open and liberal than the one he had known growing up. Conversations about personal freedom, identity, and social change were common among his peers.

Despite this influence, Hamza still maintained a strong sense of personal dignity. He avoided many of the excesses that others around him embraced. His upbringing had instilled certain boundaries within him—boundaries he rarely crossed.

That early training acted like an anchor.

It kept him from drifting too far, even when the currents around him pulled in different directions.

Yet emotionally, his sympathies were changing.

Because his friends were kind and decent people, Hamza found it difficult to accept that their identities alone could be considered sinful. Out of loyalty to them—and out of a genuine belief in compassion—he gradually began to voice support for the LGBTQ community.

For Hamza, this was not an act of rebellion against religion.

In his mind, it was simply fairness.

If love was a human emotion, he reasoned, how could it be wrong for two people to seek happiness together?

But while Hamza was wrestling with these thoughts, his parents were beginning to notice subtle changes in him.

Their conversations with their son felt different now. His tone carried new ideas, unfamiliar arguments, and questions that unsettled them deeply.

They could sense that his worldview was shifting.

For them, this was painful.

Their faith taught them that some ideas could lead a person away from the path of truth. Watching their son move toward those ideas filled them with quiet fear.

So they did what believers often do when faced with helplessness.

They prayed.

With heavy hearts, Hamza's parents turned to Allah again and again, asking for their son to be guided back to what they believed was the right path. His mother's tears often returned to the prayer mat, just as they had many years earlier.

The struggle unfolding within Hamza, however, was not simple.

It was not merely a matter of choosing one side over another.

It was a conflict between two powerful forces in his life: the faith he had inherited from his childhood, and the realities he was witnessing around him every day.

Between belief and experience.

Between tradition and modernity.

Between certainty and doubt.

And this quiet struggle slowly became the central battle of his life.

Time passed quickly, and before he realized it, Hamza had entered the final year of his graduation.

This stage of life carried a different atmosphere. Many students began thinking seriously about their futures—about careers, responsibilities, and the direction their lives would take after university.

One afternoon, Hamza was sitting with two of his close friends on campus when he overheard them discussing their future plans.

They spoke with remarkable confidence.

First, they planned to work for a few years to gain professional experience. Then they intended to get married—what society now openly recognized as a same-sex marriage. A few years after that, they hoped to build a family of their own, either by adopting a child or through surrogacy.

The conversation seemed ordinary to them.

But to Hamza, it felt like the ground beneath his thoughts had suddenly shifted.

Until that moment, his support for them had been simple and emotional. He had always believed that love, in its basic form, was just a natural human feeling. If two people cared deeply for each other, why should anyone deny them happiness?

But now, hearing them speak about marriage and children forced him to confront a reality he had never seriously considered before.

In his own family—and in all the families he had grown up around—life had always followed a familiar pattern: a husband, a wife, and children raised within that bond.

Homosexual relationships had never been part of that world.

Yet here, sitting among his friends, he was listening to plans that treated such arrangements as completely normal.

The realization unsettled him.

What troubled him most was not the idea of their relationship—it was the thought of a child growing up without a mother.

Suddenly, Hamza found his mind drifting back to the children in his own family.

He pictured his sister's children laughing and playing in the house. He remembered his elder brother's infant—barely six months old—still completely dependent on the warmth and nourishment of a mother's embrace.

The image of that tiny child resting peacefully in its mother's arms came vividly to his mind.

Could any other bond replace that?

Could anyone replicate the quiet comfort that flows naturally between a mother and her child?

The thought pierced him deeply.

He imagined a child growing up without ever knowing that tenderness—the gentle touch, the soothing voice, the silent reassurance that only a mother can give.

And for the first time, Hamza felt a profound unease.

His thoughts drifted further back into his own childhood.

He remembered the countless moments of love he had received from his mother—her quiet sacrifices, her protective care, the strength he had drawn from her presence during difficult times.

He even recalled the day he had argued with his sister for scolding her young child. At the time, he had been unable to tolerate even a small harsh word directed toward a child.

Now those memories returned with new meaning.

Slowly, Hamza began to understand something deeper.

Motherhood was not simply a social role.

It was something far more profound—a reality woven into the very emotional structure of human life.

To remove the presence of a mother from a child's upbringing suddenly seemed to him like removing one of the fundamental truths of nature itself.

The realization shook him.

It felt as though a veil was slowly lifting before his eyes.

For the first time, Hamza began to sense that the commandments of Islam might carry wisdom that was not immediately visible on the surface. Perhaps they were not merely restrictions imposed by tradition, but protections designed to preserve something deeper within human life.

Until that moment, he had been able to imagine homosexuality as simply another variation within society.

But the thought of children growing up in such arrangements—without the presence of a mother—felt impossible for him to reconcile.

And that realization marked the beginning of a new turning point in his journey.

For the first time in his life, Hamza felt as though the wisdom behind Allah's commandments was slowly unveiling itself before him.

What he had once seen as rigid restrictions now appeared in a different light. These laws, he began to realize, were not meant to suppress love or deny human happiness. They were meant to protect something deeper—the delicate harmony of human relationships, the balance of family, and the purity of the bonds that hold society together.

With this realization came a heavy wave of guilt.

Hamza felt as though he had wandered far from the path his parents had always prayed for him to follow. While his family had tried to remain steadfast in faith, he had allowed himself to be swayed by modern ideas and emotional reasoning.

The thought troubled him deeply.

How had he, the son of parents who had spent countless nights praying for his guidance, drifted so far into confusion?

He began to question himself with painful honesty. Perhaps he had been blinded by compassion—so eager to defend the feelings of others that he had failed to consider the deeper consequences of what he was supporting.

Yet even as regret settled into his heart, another realization slowly emerged.

Faith was not meant to silence questions.

Faith was meant to guide them.

Hamza began to understand that divine laws were not arbitrary commands imposed without reason. They were part of a wisdom far greater than human understanding—a wisdom designed to protect humanity even when people could not immediately see its purpose.

Still, one troubling thought continued to haunt him.

How would he face the very people in front of whom he had once defended homosexuality with such conviction?

The idea of meeting them again filled him with discomfort. But even heavier than that was another feeling—a quiet, overwhelming shame before his Creator.

More than society, more than friends or family, it was Allah before whom Hamza felt humbled.

And yet, somewhere deep within his heart, he also felt a strange sense of gratitude.

Because the clarity now forming inside him did not feel like something he had discovered on his own. It felt as though Allah Himself had lifted a veil from his eyes, guiding him gently out of confusion and back toward truth.

After many restless days and sleepless nights, Hamza finally did something he had been avoiding.

He spread his prayer mat.

For a moment he simply stood there, staring at it, feeling the weight of everything that had passed through his mind in recent months.

Then he lowered himself into sujood.

The instant his forehead touched the ground, something inside him broke open.

Tears began to flow uncontrollably.

Words escaped his lips again and again.

"Tauba... Astaghfirullah... Astaghfirullah..."

He repeated them until his voice grew weak and his breath trembled.

In that moment, every trace of pride dissolved. The stubbornness that had once fueled his arguments disappeared completely. For the first time in years, Hamza was no longer debating ideas, searching through books, or weighing intellectual arguments.

He was simply standing before his Lord—with nothing but honesty.

As his tears continued to fall, a memory from his childhood suddenly returned to him.

He saw his mother again, sitting on her prayer mat, her shoulders trembling as she cried quietly before Allah. He remembered how she used to whisper words of gratitude for even the smallest blessings. He remembered her telling him that the peace found in prayer was unlike anything the world could offer.

At the time, those words had seemed simple.

Now he finally understood them.

Lying there in prostration, Hamza felt a tranquility he had never experienced before. It was as though a great weight had been lifted from his soul. The restlessness that had once filled his mind began to fade, replaced by a calm that was deeper than any pleasure he had ever known.

It was a peace that could not be explained.

It could only be felt.

Slowly, the questions that had once tormented him began to lose their grip. The answers he had spent years chasing through books and debates now seemed almost insignificant compared to the clarity that had settled into his heart.

He realized something important in that moment.

Divine wisdom is not always uncovered through intellect alone.

Sometimes it is granted only to those who seek sincerely—and bow with humility.

As Hamza rose from prayer, he began to see his life differently.

He understood now that his parents had never truly controlled his choices. His mother could not force him to follow her advice, nor could his father shield him from every influence of the world.

But what they had given him was far more powerful than control.

They had given him a foundation.

A childhood filled with love.

An upbringing rooted in the difference between right and wrong.

A home where faith was not merely spoken about, but lived quietly every day.

Those early teachings, he now realized, had left a permanent imprint on his soul. Even when he wandered into confusion, that foundation had remained within him, silently guiding him back.

Perhaps, he thought, it was this very upbringing that had protected him from losing himself completely.

Even the intelligence that once led him into doubt now appeared to him as a blessing. It had allowed him to question, to struggle, and eventually to discover truth with greater conviction.

In a strange way, every stage of his journey had served a purpose.

The confusion. The searching. The conflict.

All of it had led him here. Hamza no longer felt like the uncertain young man who had been drifting between opposing ideas.

He felt like someone who had passed through darkness and emerged into light.

He had tasted doubt.

He had lived through inner conflict.

And now, standing on the other side of that struggle, his faith felt stronger and more deliberate than ever before.

For Hamza, this was not merely a return to religion.

It was a victory over his own nafs.

A reclaiming of his soul.

And the quiet beginning of a life in which he would strive, with humility and sincerity, to walk firmly on the path that Allah had chosen for him.

* * * * *

Chapter 2

The Dauntless Maryam

Maryam was born into the kind of family that exists in the quiet middle ground of life — not wealthy enough to be free of worry, not poor enough to be defined by it. Her father, Mr. Yunus, was the sole breadwinner, carrying the financial weight of an entire household on his shoulders: his wife, his two children, his parents, and his sister, all living together under one roof in the way that generations of Indian families had done before them. It was a home filled with the noise of shared meals, overlapping conversations, and the comfortable familiarity of people who had known each other their whole lives.

Maryam had a younger brother, Hassan — just one year her junior — close enough in age that they shared almost everything: the same childhood, the same home, the same parents. Almost everything, but not quite.

When the time came for Maryam's school admission, her mother, Mrs. Zubaida, felt the weight of the moment more deeply than anyone else in the house seemed to. To the rest of the family, it was a simple errand — find a school, fill in the forms, move on. But for Zubaida, it was something else entirely. It was a door. And she wanted it to be the right one.

She had set her heart on a good convent school — the kind of institution with discipline in its bones, quality woven into its walls, and a reputation for producing young women who could hold their own in the world. She knew what such a place could do for a girl like Maryam.

But she also knew the numbers. With Hassan only a year behind, both children would be in school simultaneously within twelve months. Two sets of high end convent fees on a single salary — it was a calculation that didn't quite add up, and she knew it even as she chose to voice her wish anyway.

She approached her husband gently, carefully, the way a woman learns to when she has lived long enough inside a household shaped by unspoken rules. She told him she wanted Maryam to have the best possible start. That she deserved it.

Mr. Yunus gave her the answer she had already written in her head before she'd even opened her mouth. The finances wouldn't stretch. It wasn't possible. Perhaps another school.

Maryam was enrolled in a basic English-medium school. Zubaida accepted it — not easily, but quietly — and turned her attention to making sure her daughter thrived wherever she was planted.

The rest of the household barely noticed the compromise that had been made. To Maryam's grandparents, her aunt, and even to Mr. Yunus himself, the whole matter had been rather unremarkable. Zubaida, they felt, had made far too much of a simple thing. Children went to school. It happened every day. Why all the emotion?

What they didn't see — or perhaps chose not to — was the quiet arithmetic of inequality that had already begun. In a home where sons and daughters were declared equal in the same breath they were treated differently, the scales had already been tipped, so gradually that no one noticed the tilting.

Then came Hassan's turn.

The house transformed. Almost overnight, it became alive with a kind of energy that had been entirely absent the year before. Maryam's admission had been a transaction. Hassan's was a celebration.

His grandparents leaned forward with interest at the dinner table, asking questions, offering opinions. His aunt and uncles debated the merits of different schools with the enthusiasm of people who had been waiting for exactly this conversation. And Mr. Yunus — Hassan's father, the same man who had told his wife that convent fees were simply out of the question — lit up with a pride so visible it filled the room.

This was different. This mattered.

School brochures were spread across tables. Fees were discussed, not as obstacles but as investments. The best school, they all agreed, was what Hassan deserved. And so it was decided — Hassan would be admitted to the most prestigious convent school in the city. Modern facilities, excellent teachers, a name that would open doors for decades to come.

The very school that had been deemed impossible for Maryam one year ago was now not only possible, but obvious for Hassan.

Mrs. Zubaida watched all of this unfold without a word. Those around her may have read her silence as acceptance, even approval. They would have been wrong.

She loved Hassan with every fibre of her being. He was her son, her child, the boy she had carried and raised and prayed over. She wanted nothing less than the world for him. But she wanted the same world for Maryam and therein lay everything.

In her heart, a quiet storm was gathering. Because love, she believed with a certainty that came from somewhere deeper than reason, was not something to be divided unequally between children based on their gender. That was not love. That was favouritism dressed in the language of love, and she refused to call it by any other name.

She had feared this moment. Now it had arrived.

She stood before her husband and spoke plainly, her voice carrying the steadiness of a woman who had already done her grieving in private. Her position was simple: either both children would attend schools of equal standing, or both would attend the convent. There was no version of this story in which one child's future was worth more than the other's. Not in her home. Not while she was their mother.

Mr. Yunus didn't hear her. Or rather, he heard the words and dismissed them — the way powerful men sometimes dismiss the voices of the women closest to them, convinced that their authority is self-evident and needs no defence. He was the provider. He was the head of this house. His decision, he made clear, was final. The dismissal landed like a blow.

That same day, Zubaida packed a bag.

She moved through the house with the calm of someone who has already made peace with a decision before acting on it. She took Maryam by the hand, and she left — walking out of that door and into her own mother's home, carrying with her nothing but her daughter and her dignity.

Her parting words were not shouted in rage. They were spoken with a quiet, devastating clarity: *"If Hassan is more loved and more valued in this house than Maryam, then keep your beloved son with you. I will not raise my daughter in a place that has already decided she is worth less."*

Mr. Yunus watched her go with an expression of mild irritation rather than alarm. She was emotional. She would cool down. Women always did. He turned to his parents, who nodded in agreement, their voices carrying the same breezy confidence of people who had never been made to question themselves.

"Come back when your mind is clear," his mother said.

His sister said nothing — only smiled the small, private smile of someone quietly pleased by another's unravelling.

And the house settled back into its noise, convinced the storm had already passed.

It had not even begun.

She left without looking back.

Not because she didn't love that home — she did, deeply and painfully — but because love without dignity is just endurance, and Zubaida had endured enough. She held Maryam's hand tightly as they walked, her grip firm and deliberate, a silent promise passed from palm to palm. She would not cry in front of her daughter. She would not let the child carry the weight of her mother's breaking heart. Whatever storm raged inside her chest, Maryam would not see it.

Her mother's house received them the way a harbour receives a battered ship — without fanfare, without judgement, with simply the quiet relief of safety. Here, at least, both she and her daughter would be seen as they were: worthy, equal, loved.

Behind her, the house she had left continued as though nothing of consequence had occurred.

A week passed.

And it was in that week that Mr. Yunus began to understand, in the most unglamorous of ways, exactly what his wife had been doing all along.

There was no breakfast waiting when he woke up. No lunch packed for the office, no warm dinner on the table when he returned. His mother and sister were present in the house — physically present — and yet somehow, inexplicably, nothing functioned. The laundry accumulated in quiet protest. He opened his wardrobe one morning to find no clean shirt for work and stood there for a long moment, staring into the evidence of his own assumptions.

He had always known, in the abstract way that comfortable people know things, that Zubaida managed the home. He simply had not understood what *managing the home* actually meant — the ten thousand invisible acts performed before sunrise and after sunset, the anticipating, the preparing, the remembering, the doing and redoing — all of it executed so seamlessly that it had appeared, to him, to require no effort at all.

Now, in her absence, the machinery of the household ground to a halt. And no one stepped in to fill the silence she had left.

Then Hassan fell ill.

The fever came suddenly and climbed quickly. The doctor confirmed a viral infection — the kind that demanded patience, careful feeding, consistent monitoring. Mr. Yunus hovered over his son with a worry he didn't know how to translate into action.

What he witnessed next unsettled him in ways he hadn't expected.

The grandmother — the same woman who had clucked and fussed over Hassan for years, who had slipped him sweets behind his mother's back and called him the light of her eyes — seemed to have quietly stepped away from the responsibility. She would look in on the boy, occasionally. But the special meals, the gentle coaxing, the kind of devoted attention a sick child needs — that had vanished. Hassan's aunt, his father's sister, was similarly occupied: mostly with her phone, scrolling through a world more interesting than the one in front of her. When Mr. Yunus asked for her help, she offered excuses with the ease of someone who had rehearsed them.

In desperation, they fed the feverish child food from outside — fried, greasy things that made his stomach revolt. When Hassan's condition worsened and he suffered through a miserable night of loose motions, no one, it turned out, wanted to deal with the aftermath. The enquiries about how he was doing grew less frequent. Then stopped altogether.

Five days of leave from the office. Twelve days since Zubaida had walked out the door.

One afternoon, at the end of his rope, Mr. Yunus went to his mother and asked her — simply, humbly — to make some khichdi for Hassan. Just khichdi. Soft rice and lentils, the most basic of comfort foods.

His mother looked at him and said, without softening her voice at all: *"Bring Zubaida back. This is her job, not mine."*

He stood very still.

Because he remembered — with a clarity that felt like cold water — that this same woman had watched Zubaida leave and called after her: *"Come back only when your mind is clear."* The condescension had been so effortless then, so assured. And now here she was, twelve days later, demanding the very woman she had dismissed.

Something shifted in Mr. Yunus in that moment. Not dramatically, not all at once — but the way a man shifts when the ground beneath a long-held belief finally gives way.

He thought about Zubaida.

He thought about the mornings she rose before anyone else stirred, moving quietly through the dark kitchen so that he would have a hot meal before work. He thought about the way she tracked both children's health with the precision of someone who understood that caring for a child is not a single act but a continuous, unending practice. He thought about how she had looked after his parents — his parents, not hers — cooking for them, respecting them, serving them, with no obligation under Islamic teachings to do any of it, and yet doing it all anyway, out of nothing but the generosity of her character.

He had taken every single bit of it for granted.

A man provides money, yes. But money does not cook the meals or soothe the sick child or hold the household together when everything pulls it apart. Behind every functioning home is a woman whose labour is invisible precisely because she performs it so well. He had confused her competence for effortlessness, and her silence for contentment.

Then he noticed his own hands trembling slightly. He pressed them to his forehead. He was warm.

He checked his temperature. The fever had crossed him too, passed from his son's small body into his own. Now both of them lay in that disordered house — sick, unattended, and utterly helpless.

He picked up the phone.

When Zubaida answered, he didn't reach for excuses or justifications. There were none left that he could believe in himself. His voice, when it came, was stripped of all the authority he had worn so proudly.

"Please come home, Zubaida. This house is only complete with you. Without you, there is no peace here — no warmth, no order, nothing. I am sorry. I am truly sorry."

He told her about Hassan. He told her about his own fever. And then he said the words she had been asking for all along — not as a concession, but as a promise: *"I will admit Maryam and Hassan to the convent school together. You have my word."*

On the other end of the line, Zubaida closed her eyes.

She had not left to punish him. She had left because staying would have meant teaching her daughter that injustice was something women simply absorbed. She had fought quietly, without bitterness, without cruelty — only with the one weapon available to a woman who has run out of words: her absence. And it had spoken louder than anything she could have said.

For the first time in her married life, she felt heard. Truly, properly heard. She exhaled — long and slow — and the tightness that had lived in her chest for twelve days began, at last, to loosen.

She went home.

Both children were enrolled in the convent school that term, just as he had promised.

And life, with the particular grace it sometimes offers after a storm, moved forward.

Zubaida poured herself into raising them — not just feeding and clothing them, but *shaping* them, pressing her values into the soft clay of their characters with the patience of someone who understood that a mother's real work is never the work anyone can see. Mr. Yunus, humbled and changed, worked harder than before — not to assert his authority, but to honour the promise he had made and the family he had nearly broken.

Maryam blossomed. She had always been bright, but at the convent school she discovered the full extent of what she was capable of. Academically, she excelled beyond Hassan, though Hassan had gifts of his own — a natural athlete, competitive and spirited, the kind of boy who came home with muddy knees and trophies in equal measure. But Maryam found her voice. Literally. She stepped onto the stage for the first time at a school debate and something lit up inside her that never quite went out. Quizzes, debates, inter-school speech competitions, you name them — she collected medals with the quiet determination of someone proving something not to the world, but to herself.

Her grandfather favoured Hassan in the way that grandfathers of his generation sometimes did, indulging the boy in ways he never thought to indulge the girl. Maryam noticed. She had learned early, from watching her mother, that the world would not always treat her fairly — and that the only answer to that was to become undeniable. So she worked on herself with patience. And she grew.

Years passed in the rhythm of school terms and growing heights and parents who watched their children with the private pride of people who had sacrificed in ways their children would perhaps never fully know.

And then came the day that made every sacrifice feel, suddenly and completely, worth it.

Maryam received her admission letter.

Not just any college — one of the finest medical institutions in the country, a place that thousands of students aimed for and most never reached. The girl who had once been enrolled in a school by a mother fighting alone for her right to a fair start was now standing at the entrance of a future that stretched further than even that mother had dared to dream.

Mrs. Zubaida held the letter in her hands for a long time.

She didn't say much. She didn't need to.

Mr. Yunus had changed. Not overnight, and not without the kind of quiet reckoning that leaves a mark on a man — but he had changed, and those who knew him well could see it in the smallest things. The way he paused before speaking. The way he turned to his wife now, not as a formality, but out of genuine need for her counsel. The decisions of the household that had once been handed down from on high were now discussed, weighed, and made together.

He told her often — and he meant it each time — *"You are not only a wonderful companion, but an exceptional mother."* It was not flattery. It was the hard-won recognition of a man who had once taken everything for granted and had been shown, in no uncertain terms, exactly what that cost.

When Maryam's acceptance letter arrived from one of the country's finest medical colleges, Mr. Yunus held it and felt something he hadn't expected: humility. This was not just his daughter's triumph. It was Zubaida's. Every early morning, every patient hour of revision, every quiet word of encouragement that had built Maryam's confidence brick by brick — that was her mother's work. He knew it, and he said so.

And then, a year later, Hassan followed.

Two children. Two medical students. One household that had once been on the verge of fracturing over the price of school fees now stood overflowing with a joy it could barely contain. Mr. Yunus looked at his wife and said, his voice thick with something that sat between pride and gratitude: *"Because of you, there will soon be two doctors in this home. Had it not been for your wisdom, old ignorant traditions might have held Maryam back from everything she was always capable of becoming."*

He said *ignorant traditions*. He said it plainly, without flinching. And Zubaida, who had fought for exactly this acknowledgement without ever asking for it, simply smiled — the deep, settled smile of a woman who has lived long enough to see the truth vindicated.

By the time Maryam walked the corridors of her medical college, she had grown into herself completely.

She was sharp, yes — academically brilliant in the way that draws the attention of professors who have taught for decades and can recognise genuine talent when it sits in front of them. But it wasn't only her intellect that made her stand out. It was the quality of her presence. There was a warmth to Maryam, an openness that made people feel at ease around her — classmates sought her out when they were struggling, not just for notes but for reassurance, and she gave both freely. She moved through that demanding environment with a grace that seemed effortless, though anyone who knew her story would understand that it had been carefully cultivated, year after year.

It was in this setting that Adeel first noticed her.

He noticed her the way one notices something that has always been there but suddenly comes into focus — not with a single dramatic moment, but through accumulation. The way she spoke in seminars, confident without being overbearing. The way she laughed with her friends, fully and without self-consciousness. The way she treated everyone — from professors to the quietest student in the back row — with the same genuine courtesy.

He was drawn to all of it. But what held his attention, what made his admiration deepen into something more serious, was the dignity with which she carried herself. In a world that often rewards loudness, Maryam's quiet assurance was arresting.

He began, in his own understated way, to show her who he was.

He was not the kind of young man who announced his feelings through grand performances. His affection expressed itself in small, careful acts — the kind that only a person paying close attention would notice. He would arrive early to a lecture and quietly secure the best seat, leaving it for her without drawing attention to the gesture. He spoke to her and her friends with a courtesy that felt natural rather than performed. He maintained a respectful distance that, paradoxically, communicated more regard for her than any overture could have. With the female professors, with his classmates, with everyone — he conducted himself with a maturity that sat unusually well on young shoulders.

Maryam noticed. She noticed everything.

She had grown up watching her mother navigate a world that did not always treat women fairly, and in doing so she had developed an instinct for character — a finely tuned ability to distinguish between men who respected women and men who merely performed respect when it was convenient.

Adeel, she understood quite quickly, was the former. There was a sincerity to him that she trusted before she had words for why.

Cricket was another dimension of him that she came to admire — not the sport itself, but what it revealed about him. He played with commitment and sportsmanship, the kind of player his teammates rallied around. Watching him on the field, focused and alive, she saw the same quality that made him good in every other context: he showed up, fully, for the things he cared about.

When he finally gathered the courage to tell her — his voice unsteady, his intentions unmistakable — she already knew. She had known for a while. She said yes with a smile that held no hesitation, only the quiet happiness of someone arriving somewhere they had been moving toward without quite realising it.

Their wedding was only days away.

Adeel walked through those final days in a state of wondering disbelief — not the anxious kind, but the kind that comes from receiving something you had hoped for but never quite allowed yourself to expect. Maryam had no shortage of admirers; he was not unaware of this. She was accomplished, beautiful, and possessed of a quality of soul that drew people toward her without her ever trying. That she had chosen *him* — this fact sat in his chest like a warm, steady light.

He thought about their future with a seriousness that felt good rather than heavy. He wanted to be worthy of her. Not in the way of performance or proving, but in the quiet daily way of a man who understands what he has been given and intends to honour it. Their bond, he felt, was built on something real — mutual respect, shared values, the kind of admiration that had grown slowly and was therefore unlikely to fade quickly.

He was, in the truest sense of the word, grateful.

And so the preparations began.

Both households came alive with the beautiful chaos of a wedding in the making. Relatives arrived in clusters, neighbours stopped by with congratulations that lingered into long visits, and the rooms filled with the overlapping noise of planning — guest lists, menu, fabrics, jewellery, flowers. The smell of traditional food drifted through the corridors. Laughter erupted without warning. Everyone, it seemed, had an opinion and was delighted to share it.

Maryam moved through it all with her characteristic composure, though privately she had always imagined something quieter for herself. A simple ceremony, she had thought — intimate, meaningful, where the weight of the occasion rested on the vows rather than the venue. She had voiced this wish, gently, more than once. But families have their own momentum, and this one had been waiting a long time for a celebration.

Neither her family nor Adeel's would hear of simplicity. There were expectations to meet, relatives to honour, a social world that would be watching and would remember. Maryam understood this, even if she didn't entirely share it, and she let her preference go with the graceful acceptance of someone who has learned to choose her battles.

Her father, above all, was immovable on this point.

Mr. Yunus had spent years making up for lost ground — years of learning, correcting, rebuilding. And now his daughter, his brilliant Maryam who had become a doctor, who had stood on stages and collected medals and made his heart swell with a pride. He would not send her into this new life quietly. He would send her like the princess she had always been, whether or not the family had always treated her as one.

He poured himself into every detail: the venue, the decorations, the clothes, the jewellery that caught the light when she walked. He wanted guests to leave talking about it for years. He wanted the world to see what his daughter was worth.

When the day finally arrived, it was everything he had envisioned — magnificent, warm, and alive with the joy of people who had gathered to celebrate something genuinely worth celebrating.

In the midst of it all, Mr. Yunus found his wife's eyes across the room.

No words were needed. They had lived too much together for that.

A wedding, at its heart, is never just about two people.

It is the visible surface of everything that came before — every sacrifice made in quiet rooms, every argument weathered, every small act of love that went unwitnessed. Maryam's wedding carried all of that history within it, even if the guests who admired the decorations and praised the food had no way of knowing. Mr. Yunus knew. Mrs. Zubaida knew. And between the two of them, in the unspoken language of people who have lived through something together, the evening held a meaning that no amount of floral arrangements could fully express.

The first year of marriage moved gently for Adeel and Maryam, the way first years do when two people are still discovering the pleasure of being chosen by someone they admire.

They took evening walks that stretched longer than intended, conversations carrying them past the point of tiredness. They visited parks on quiet afternoons, went for dinners on occasions that needed no special reason, and took small trips that accumulated into a private geography of shared memory. These were ordinary things — but in the accumulation of ordinary things, a life is built, and both of them understood this.

They were considerate people, and it showed. They brought gifts home for their families without being asked, the small thoughtful kind that said *I was thinking of you* without making a performance of it. Maryam, in particular, moved into her new family with the same intention she brought to everything — she wanted to belong, genuinely. She helped in the kitchen, sat with her mother-in-law Mrs. Haleema for long unhurried conversations, and treated every member of the household with a respect that was not manufactured but felt. Slowly, she wove herself into the fabric of the home.

Guests who visited Mrs. Haleema could not help but notice Maryam. Her beauty, certainly, but more than that — the quality of her presence, the way she spoke, the quiet maturity with which she held herself in a room full of people making assessments. She was praised openly, the way people in Indian households sometimes praise with a warmth that is genuine but not always considered in its consequences.

On one such occasion, a neighbour, clearly impressed, remarked that Adeel had been extraordinarily fortunate —

that he had found a wife, in her estimation, rather better than what he deserved.

It was the kind of casual observation that people offer without much thought. But words land differently depending on who receives them.

Mrs. Haleema received this one badly.

She was not a cruel woman. But she was a mother — the particular kind of mother for whom a son's worth is a matter of personal honour. The suggestion that Maryam had somehow made the better bargain touched something territorial in her. She responded with a sharpness that the gathering did not quite expect — reminding the neighbour that Adeel was a doctor, a man of exceptional quality, handsome and accomplished, and that Maryam, if she had searched the world, could not have done better. She added, with a possessiveness that revealed more than she intended, that Maryam had been rather clever in securing him during their student years, as though she had recognised his value early and moved accordingly.

The room absorbed this in the way rooms absorb uncomfortable moments — with a slight shift, a readjustment of expressions, and then a careful return to lighter subjects.

But something had been said that could not be unsaid, and somewhere in that room, a seed had been planted.

Adeel loved Maryam with a sincerity that was not performative. He trusted her in the way that people trust those they have chosen deliberately and observed carefully — with a deep, quiet certainty. In the early months, when his mother began to make small remarks — a comment here, a doubt there — he deflected them with patience, explaining to her that she was misreading Maryam, that Maryam was not who she was imagining her to be. He knew his wife. He stood by what he knew.

But repetition is a quiet and relentless force. A single doubt, voiced once, is easy to dismiss. Voiced again and again, in different forms, by people whose love you do not question — it begins to work on you in ways you don't notice until the work is already done.

His mother and sister were not wicked women. But they were, in the way of people who feel displaced by someone else's light, unsettled by Maryam. She was too admired. Too accomplished. In a household where they had been the centre, she created a new gravity — and they found themselves orbiting it uncomfortably. The comments grew more frequent. The doubts more specific. The portrait they painted of Maryam, stroked one small detail at a time, began to look less and less like the woman Adeel had married.

And Adeel, who loved them, who had grown up trusting their judgement, began — without fully knowing it — to see through a lens that had been quietly handed to him.

The arguments that had once dissolved in laughter now had edges. Problems that would have passed in an hour were carried forward into the next day, and the day after. The lightness between them grew heavier. And from outside the marriage, Mrs. Haleema and her daughter offered commentary that did not help — telling Maryam, with the particular confidence of women who believe tradition is on their side, that whatever respect she commanded in her hospital was entirely separate from what was expected of her at home. That at home, she owed obedience.

Maryam heard these words. She felt where they landed.

She was a woman who understood herself well enough to know when something was unjust, and perceptive enough to see exactly what was happening around her. But she was also someone whose faith ran deeper than her grievance. She believed in her marriage. She believed that love, when it was real, was worth the effort of preservation — and she believed, with a quiet certainty that came not from naivety but from genuine conviction, that Allah honoured those who strove to keep what mattered intact.

So she made a decision that cost her something.

She would try harder. Not because she was wrong, but because she valued what she was trying to save more than she valued being right. She turned toward Adeel with more tenderness, not less. She listened more carefully, accommodated more willingly, and when her heart rose in protest — because it often did — she stilled it with the reminder that marriage is not a transaction of equal effort but a practice of continuous, sometimes unreciprocated, giving.

She pressed her own needs quieter.

She told herself this was wisdom.

She told herself this was faith.

She was not entirely wrong. But she was not entirely right either — and the difference between the two would become important later.

For a while, the peace held.

Maryam's efforts appeared to bear fruit — the arguments grew less frequent, the atmosphere at home softened, and Adeel seemed more settled. She allowed herself to believe, cautiously, that the worst had passed. That her patience had worked its quiet miracle.

But she had misread the situation, and the misreading would cost her.

Adeel had not understood her sacrifices for what they were — acts of love from a woman trying to save something precious. He had interpreted them as confirmation of what his mother and sister had been telling him all along: that a wife needed managing. That firmness worked. That the right balance of authority kept a household in order. Maryam's softening, her compliance, her willingness to bend — he had filed all of it under the wrong heading. And so, almost without noticing, the tenderness in him began to be replaced by something harder. Something that looked, from the outside, like confidence, but felt, from the inside of their marriage, like control.

The man who had once reserved a seat for her quietly, who had treated her with a courtesy that made her feel genuinely seen — that man was still there, somewhere. But he was increasingly difficult to reach.

Maryam felt the shift the way one feels a change in temperature — not in a single moment, but in the gradual, undeniable accumulation of small things. The warmth between them had not disappeared entirely, but it had been overlaid with something else. Pressure where there had once been tenderness. Expectation where there had once been care. She buried her disappointment in the only way she knew how — by working harder, both at the hospital and at home — and carried on.

One night there was an emergency call from the hospital.

It was past midnight when her phone rang. A major accident. Multiple casualties. Her presence in the operating theatre was needed immediately. She was a surgeon — this was the life she had chosen, and she had chosen it with full knowledge of what it demanded. She was out of the door within minutes.

The surgery was long and unrelenting, the kind that takes everything from you and leaves nothing in reserve. It stretched through the night and into the pale hours of the morning, and when it was finally over, Maryam had nothing left. She found the small rest room off the corridor, lay down for what she intended to be a few minutes, and fell into the deep, involuntary sleep of complete exhaustion.

When she opened her eyes, the light through the window was wrong. Too warm. Too late.

Four in the afternoon.

She sat up with a jolt, her mind immediately calculating — her evening OPD began in two hours. She moved quickly, gathered herself, and drove home to freshen up before returning. The whole drive back, she thought of nothing except the practicalities of the next few hours.

She was not prepared for what met her at the door.

No one asked if she was alright. No one asked about the surgery, or the patient, or the hours she had spent on her feet in a theatre while the rest of the household slept. Instead, she walked into cold expressions and colder words.

Mrs. Haleema had, in the early days of the marriage, spoken of Maryam's career with pride — had mentioned it to neighbours and relatives with the satisfaction of a woman who felt her family had elevated itself. *Both my son and daughter-in-law are doctors.* She had said it often, and she had meant it.

But somewhere along the way, pride had curdled into something uglier. Maryam's reputation at the hospital had grown. Her name was known. Patients requested her. Colleagues respected her. And in the arithmetic of Mrs. Haleema's affections, where Adeel's worth was always the fixed point around which everything else was measured, this had become a problem. Her daughter-in-law's success now cast a shadow that she hadn't anticipated and couldn't comfortably stand in.

So she spoke. She taunted. She questioned Maryam's dedication to the home, her priorities, her character. And then, reaching for the sharpest instrument available, she turned her words toward Maryam's mother — toward Zubaida, who was not in that room, who had no idea any of this was happening — and suggested that she had failed to raise her daughter properly.

Across the room, Adeel stood and said nothing.

His silence was its own kind of wound.

He was a doctor. He understood better than anyone in that room what an emergency surgery demanded — the hours, the focus, the physical toll, the particular emptiness that follows when it is over. He had lived that himself. And he knew Maryam. He had known her since their student days, had chosen her precisely because of her integrity, her seriousness, her fundamental decency. Every word his mother was saying was a distortion, and somewhere beneath the surface of his compliance, he knew it.

But knowledge and courage are not the same thing.

It is a painful truth that some men, entrusted by Allah with the role of *qawwam* — the protector, the maintainer, the one who stands in front — choose to hold tightly to the privileges of that position while quietly setting down its responsibilities. They receive the honour of the title but excuse themselves from its demands: to protect, to be just, to stand between their wife and harm even when the harm comes from within their own family. It requires a particular kind of courage to look at the people you love and tell them they are wrong. Adeel did not find that courage in this moment. He found, instead, the easier path — silence before his family, and the release of his discomfort later, onto his wife.

When Maryam's name was blackened, he stayed quiet. But when Maryam, her voice shaking with a pain she could no longer contain, finally spoke — when she asked why her mother, who knew nothing of these walls or these arguments, was being dragged into every conflict — Adeel turned on her. Not on his mother. On his wife. He raised his voice, he asserted himself, he shut her down with the kind of authority that requires no justification because it has never been asked to provide any.

The room settled. Order, of a certain kind, was restored.

And Maryam stood in the middle of it, a woman who had come home from saving a life, and understood completely what had just been saved, and what had not.

She knew what was being whispered.

The surgery had ended at eleven in the morning — why had she only arrived home at four? The question moved through the household like smoke, finding its way into every corner. In the hospital there was a colleague who admired her work and made no secret of his professional respect for her. Adeel had noticed this, and it had settled inside him as an unease he could neither name precisely nor let go of entirely. The whispers at home now gave that unease a shape.

But Maryam was not that woman. She had never been that woman.

She had grown up knowing that she was admired — she was not without self-awareness — and from her earliest years she had understood that admiration was not an invitation. After her marriage, she remained entirely conscious of the glances and the attention, and she turned away from all of it with a deliberateness rooted not in effort but in conviction. Her loyalty to Adeel was absolute. And above all of that, beyond every human calculation, was her certainty that Allah sees. Everything. Always. The intention behind the act, the truth behind the appearance, the contents of every heart that believes itself unobserved. She did not need anyone in that house to believe her. She needed only to remain who she was before the One who already knew.

She went to her room.

The tears came the way they come when they have been held back too long — without warning and without restraint. She cancelled the evening OPD. Not because she couldn't bear the work, but because she needed, for a few hours, to put down everything she was carrying and stand somewhere quiet.

She made her ablution slowly, with the deliberateness of someone preparing for something important. She unrolled her prayer mat, faced the *qibla*, and stood before Allah.

She prayed for a long time.

In *sujood* — her forehead pressed to the ground, the position of deepest surrender — she stayed. The words she could not say to anyone in that house she said here, in the only conversation where she never had to translate herself, never had to justify herself, never had to be anything other than exactly who she was: a woman in pain, asking for help from the One whose help does not depend on being deserved.

The room outside was full of noise and suspicion and the residue of cruelty.

In here, there was only quiet. And in the quiet, something steadied.

In the stillness of her room, with the prayer mat still beneath her and the last traces of her tears drying on her face, Maryam began to ask herself questions.

Not the kind asked in anger, not the kind that circle without landing — but honest, searching questions, the kind a person only finds the courage for when they have stopped performing composure and allowed themselves to simply sit with the truth.

Have I ever disrespected Adeel, or his parents?

She considered it carefully, without the instinct to flatter herself. She had argued — yes. There had been moments of raised voices and poorly chosen words, the inevitable friction of two people navigating a difficult season. But disrespect? The deliberate diminishing of another's dignity? She searched herself honestly and found nothing. No.

When they faced hardship — any of them — did I ever step back?

She thought of the times she had quietly absorbed burdens that were never hers to carry. The extra effort, the swallowed grievances, the needs she had anticipated and met before they were even voiced. No. She had not stepped back. She had stepped forward, every time, even when no one noticed and no one thanked her.

Have I ever humiliated Adeel the way he humiliated me today — in front of others, with raised voice and public contempt?

The answer came quickly, and it was the same. No. Even at her most hurt, even when her words had shaken with the effort of containing everything she felt, she had never tried to diminish him before others. She had protected him, the way you protect someone you love, the way the Quran describes spouses — as garments for one another, covering what should be covered, preserving what deserves preservation.

And then the harder question. The one she had been circling.

Has Adeel made the same effort? Has he endured from my family what I have endured from his? Has he given me, consistently and freely, the respect and love I have continued to give him despite everything?

The silence that answered her was not ambiguous.

No. No. No.

She had loved him. She wanted to be clear about that, even sitting alone in the wreckage of the day — she had loved him genuinely, had chosen him with her whole self, had believed in who he was and who they could be together. But love, she was understanding now with a clarity that felt less like heartbreak and more like the lifting of a fog, love could not survive as a single-sided practice indefinitely. It was not weakness that had brought her to this point. It was the accumulated evidence of a woman who had given everything and been shown, repeatedly and without apology, that it was not enough — not because she lacked anything, but because the person receiving it had stopped seeing it.

The more she had given, the less it had been valued. The more she had softened, the harder he had become. She had interpreted her own patience as devotion. She was beginning to understand that it had also, inadvertently, taught him that there were no consequences for how he treated her.

And then the question she had been most afraid to ask arrived, quietly, and waited.

Should I continue this marriage?

She let it sit. She did not rush toward an answer or retreat from the question. She sat with it the way one sits with something important, giving it the weight it deserved.

Her heart answered without drama or fury. Simply, and with a finality that surprised her with its gentleness:

No.

What followed was not grief. That is what surprised her most.

She had expected, when this moment came — if it came — to feel the ground disappear beneath her. She had expected the fear of starting over, the mourning of what had been, the terrifying openness of a future unwritten. Instead, what moved through her was something she had almost forgotten the feeling of.

Peace.

A deep, unhurried, cellular peace, as though something that had been held at an unnatural angle inside her had finally been allowed to rest in its proper position. The weight she had been carrying — not just today, not just this month, but across the slow accumulation of a marriage that had been quietly diminishing her — she felt it lift. Not entirely, not all at once, but enough. Enough to breathe differently.

She thanked Allah — sincerely, from the deepest part of herself — for the mercy of *khula*. That in His infinite wisdom, He had not left women without a door. That when a marriage becomes a cage, when endurance crosses the line from virtue into self-destruction, there exists within Islam a sanctioned, dignified path to freedom. She had always known this intellectually. Tonight she understood it with her whole being.

Her decision had not been made in anger. Anger had been present earlier — it had flared when her mother's name was used as a weapon, had tightened her throat and shaken her voice. But that was not what had brought her here. What had brought her here was clarity. Quiet, prayer-wrought, honest clarity. The difference mattered to her enormously.

She began, cautiously at first and then with growing steadiness, to think forward.

Her career. The trajectory she had been building with such dedication, that she had never allowed even the most difficult days at home to derail — there was room in it still, more room than she had allowed herself to imagine in the constrained mental space of a struggling marriage. There were goals she had deferred, ambitions she had quietly set aside in the interest of keeping peace. She retrieved them now, one by one, and looked at them again with new eyes.

There was no bitterness in this accounting. No desire to punish or be vindicated. Only a woman, sitting in the reclaimed space of her own future, making plans.

The question that remained was her parents.

She thought of them for a long time — her father, who had sent her into this marriage like a princess, who had stood at that wedding with a pride so full it had barely fit inside his expression. Her mother, who had fought quietly and at great personal cost so that Maryam would have every opportunity, who had raised her daughter to know her own worth and to never settle for less.

They knew nothing of what these walls had contained.

Maryam had kept it that way deliberately, and not out of shame. She had believed — she still believed — that the interior of a marriage belongs to the two people inside it. Islam had given her the language for this: spouses as garments for one another, each covering the other's vulnerabilities with the fabric of loyalty. She had honoured that. She had not gone home after arguments to perform her grievances for an audience. She had not recruited her parents as witnesses to Adeel's failings.

But now the garment was being removed. And she would need to tell them why.

She was still sitting with this — how to begin, what to say, how to carry the weight of their shock without breaking under it herself — when the door opened.

Adeel walked in.

He did not look at her with remorse. He looked at her with the expression of a man who has decided that the disruption of the day was her fault and has arrived to deposit that conclusion. He said what he always said, in the way he always said it — blame imposed on Maryam with the casual confidence of someone who has never seriously considered that he might be wrong.

Then he changed his clothes, lay down, and went to sleep.

He slept with the ease of a man who had decided, as he had decided many times before, that things would smooth over in a day or two. That Maryam would absorb this the way she had absorbed everything else. That tomorrow the household would resume its rhythms and the incident would be filed, like all the others, under the heading of *her sensitivity*.

He did not know — could not have known, looking at her sitting quietly in that room — that she had already, entirely and without spectacle, left him. Not the house. Not yet. But the place inside her where he had lived — the place that had held his image, their memories, the future she had once imagined for them — that place was empty now. Quietly, completely, and without return.

He was, to her, simply another person in the room.

The next morning, she packed a suitcase.

She did it methodically, without tears, without the trembling hands of someone who is not sure. She folded each item with the deliberateness of a woman who knows exactly what she is doing and has made her peace with it.

When Adeel saw the suitcase, something passed through his face — a brief, involuntary flash of something that might have been fear, or the sudden recognition that this time was different. But it passed quickly, replaced by the familiar armour of pride. He did not ask her to stay. He did not look at what he had done and reckon with it.

He picked up his phone and called her father.

Adeel's voice, when he called Mr. Yunus, carried the particular bitterness of a man who believes his anger to be entirely justified.

He spoke in accusations — Maryam was selfish, she cared only for herself, she had disrespected his family and dragged their honour through the mud. His tone was that of someone filing a complaint, expecting the other side to receive it with appropriate shame. And then, with a dismissiveness that revealed everything about how little he understood the situation he had created, he said: *"Your daughter is coming back to you. Take care of her. And don't send her back until she has learned her lesson."*

He hung up and returned to his certainty that things would resolve themselves in the usual way. She would go. She would cool down. She would come back.

What he did not understand was that Maryam had already taken the most significant step of her liberation. The suitcase was simply the outward expression of a departure that had already happened, quietly, in a room where only she and Allah had been present.

Her parents received her the way they had always received her — with love that asked no questions before offering itself. But in the days that followed, as the full picture emerged in the careful, measured way that Maryam shared it, the love in that house became something steelier. Something with a spine.

They knew their daughter. They had known her as the child who turned disadvantage into discipline, who had stood on stages and collected trophies and then come home and helped her mother in the kitchen without being asked. They knew her temperament — not given to exaggeration, not easily broken, not the kind of woman who walked away from things she valued without having first tried every other option available to her. When Maryam told them she was done, they did not ask her to reconsider. Her brother,

Hassan — now himself a doctor, shaped by the same mother who had shaped Maryam — stood beside his sister without hesitation.

They formed a quiet wall around her, not of anger, but of certainty.

She will move forward. We will make sure of it.

Meanwhile, in the house Maryam had left, Adeel discovered something he had not anticipated.

Silence.

Not the ordinary silence of an evening at home, but the particular silence of an absence that fills every room it touches. He would reach, automatically, for a shared moment — to tell her something, to hear her voice — and find nothing there. He had taken her presence so thoroughly for granted that he hadn't realised, until it was gone, how much of his daily life had been quietly organised around it.

The hospital became its own kind of torment. They worked in the same building, and the distance between their paths felt both enormous and insufficient. Once, fate arranged them in the same corridor. He saw her before she saw him, and he felt something leap in his chest — recognition, longing, the involuntary hope of a man who has not yet accepted his own role in what happened.

Then she saw him.

She looked at him for the length of a breath — no warmth, no anger, no residue of what they had been — and then she walked on. As though he were simply another face in a busy corridor. A stranger.

That glance — or rather, the complete absence of anything in it — undid something in Adeel that all the arguments and silences before it had not. He stood in the corridor after she had gone and understood, perhaps for the first time with his whole self rather than just his mind, that something had ended.

Then came the rumour. It moved through the hospital the way news moves through closed communities — quickly, unstoppably, and with embellishment at every telling. Dr. Maryam had been offered a position at a prestigious hospital in the United States. She was resigning. She was leaving.

His colleagues, unaware of the depth of the fracture, were cheerful about it in the way colleagues are — teasing him that he'd be following her to America soon, asking senior doctors whether Adeel had plans to join her, making the easy assumptions of people who had seen them together and assumed that what they saw was still intact.

Adeel had no answers. He stood inside these conversations with the hollow steadiness of someone performing normality while everything inside them has shifted. The fear that had been building — the dawning, unwelcome recognition of what he stood to lose — crystallised in those interactions into something acute and undeniable.

She was not waiting. She was not cooling down. She was building forward, the way she had always built — with direction and conviction and no backward glances.

He began to understand, in the painful and belated way of someone who required loss to develop sight, what Maryam had been.

Not just his wife. Not just the woman whose compliance he had mistaken for weakness, whose sacrifices he had catalogued as expectation rather than gift. She had been — he saw it now with a clarity that came too late and cost too much — someone rare. Talented and beautiful, yes, but it was never really that. It was her quality of soul. The loyalty that had remained constant even as he tested it. The dignity she had maintained even when he had not afforded her, his own. The integrity that had been so consistent, so unperformative, that he had simply stopped registering it as something to be valued.

He had been handed something extraordinary and had spent considerable energy trying to diminish it. He had listened to voices that were smaller than her and allowed them to reshape his vision of who she was. He had chosen the comfort of his family's approval over the health of the most important relationship in his life — and in doing so, he had not protected his family. He had only lost his wife.

The void she left was not dramatic. It was simply total.

Two months after she had walked out with her suitcase, Adeel rang the doorbell of her parents' house.

He had spent those two months constructing a version of events that allowed him to arrive with hope. Surely her silence was anger, and anger faded. Surely her family — her father, her mother — would be doing what families did, gently guiding their daughter back toward her marriage, reminding her of her duties, coaxing her toward reconciliation. This was what he had grown up seeing. This was how it went.

He had convinced himself that if he arrived with sincerity, with a genuine apology and the right words, Maryam would hear him. She was reasonable. She had always been reasonable. She would see that he had understood his mistakes and she would come home.

He pressed the bell, his heart loud in his chest.

The door opened, and there was Mrs. Zubaida.

He greeted her — *Assalamu alaikum* — with the careful politeness of someone hoping to be received warmly, hoping for some sign that the ground ahead was navigable.

Her response was correct. Proper. And entirely without warmth.

Walaikum assalam.

She stepped back, gestured toward the living room, and left him there without another word. No tea offered. No enquiries about his health, his parents, the drive over. Nothing of the woman who had always treated him as an extension of her own family.

Adeel sat down in a room that felt different than he remembered it and tried to order his thoughts.

He still did not fully understand what was happening. The architecture of his assumptions remained largely intact — he was here, he was sorry, this would be resolved. The possibility that Mrs. Zubaida's coldness was not temporary displeasure but permanent reckoning did not seriously present itself to him.

Inside, Zubaida went to her daughter's room. She sat with Maryam for a moment and then spoke — not with the trembling, conflicted voice of a mother torn between her daughter's happiness and social expectation, but with the level, clear tone of a woman who had done her own reckoning long before this day arrived.

"Adeel is here. Go and meet him. Whatever decision you need to make — make it. Don't let this drag on. Close this chapter and move forward with your life."

No persuasion. No *perhaps give it one more chance* or *think of what people will say* or *marriage requires sacrifice.* None of the lines that daughters in these situations are so often handed by the very people who should be protecting them. Just clarity. Just the quiet, unambiguous message that her daughter's peace mattered more than the appearance of a marriage that had long since stopped resembling one.

Maryam heard her mother's words and felt, again, that particular quality of love that had shaped her entire life — the love that did not ask her to make herself smaller to fit a space that was not worthy of her.

She stood up, steadied herself, and walked toward the living room.

Adeel rose when she entered and began speaking immediately — the words tumbling out with the urgency of a man who is afraid that if he leaves space, the wrong thing will fill it.

"Forget everything that happened. It's been months. Let's just go home — that house has no life in it without you."

He said it with longing. He also said it with the unconscious entitlement of a man who has decided that the conclusion of this conversation is already written, and that his arrival here was the last required step.

He was waiting for her to soften. For the version of Maryam he had come here to find — the patient, accommodating, endlessly forgiving Maryam — to appear and release them both from the difficulty of this moment.

He had forgotten, entirely, who she had become.

Or perhaps he had never quite understood who she had always been.

Her parents in the meantime also entered the room.

Adeel registered this and recalibrated quickly, deciding that what he needed was privacy — the space to speak to Maryam without witnesses, to find the version of her that he was sure still existed beneath whatever had hardened around her. He turned to her father and asked if he might speak with his wife alone.

Mr. Yunus looked at him steadily. When he spoke, his voice carried no hostility — only the flat, unambiguous certainty of a man who has already done his grieving and arrived at the other side of it.

"That time has passed. Whatever decision is made here today will be made openly, in front of all of us."

The confidence Adeel had carried through the door began, quietly, to dissolve.

He looked around the room — at Mr. Yunus, at Mrs. Zubaida, at the unified stillness of a family that had clearly already decided something — and felt the first real chill of understanding. This was not the atmosphere of people waiting to be persuaded. This was the atmosphere of people who had already arrived somewhere and were simply waiting for the formalities to catch up.

Decision. They kept using that word. He turned it over, trying to fit it into the narrative he had brought with him, and found that it didn't fit at all.

Then Maryam stood up.

He watched her cross to the drawer — her hands trembling slightly, but her steps unwavering — and take out a set of papers. She walked toward him with the measured quiet of someone performing an act they have rehearsed in their mind many times and placed them on the surface in front of him.

"Now that you're here," she said, her voice low and entirely steady, *"please sign these peacefully."*

The world, for Adeel, seemed to tilt.

He stared at the papers. He looked up at her face, searching desperately for something — hesitation, doubt, the flicker of a woman who was not entirely sure. He found nothing of the kind. He looked back at the papers.

"What are you doing, Maryam?" His voice cracked at the edges. *"Who ends a marriage over something like this? Have you lost your senses?"*

Inside her chest, a bitter, wordless answer: *So this is all it was to you. My humiliation. My endurance. A small matter.*

She did not say it. She simply looked at him and repeated, with the same unshaking quiet: *"Please sign these and leave."*

He couldn't bear the stillness of her.

The Maryam he had prepared himself to face — emotional, perhaps tearful, the Maryam who had always eventually softened — was not in this room. In her place was someone he recognised in the way one recognises a person who has made a permanent decision: completely, and without the exits that anger leaves open.

Something in him broke sideways into rage.

He turned to her parents, his voice rising, filling the room with the particular sound of a man whose pride has been publicly injured and who does not know any response to that except volume. *"Do you see this? Look at your daughter — this arrogance, this stubbornness! I came here with love, to bring her home, to reconcile — and she hands me divorce papers! And you sit here and say nothing?"*

Mrs. Zubaida had spent a lifetime absorbing the noise that men make when they feel their authority slipping. She was not frightened by it. She was not even particularly moved.

"Enough." Her voice cut through his cleanly. *"You will speak calmly in this house, or you will not speak at all."*

The room contracted around his outburst. He deflated — not entirely, but enough.

When he spoke again, the rage had become something more exposed. Desperation, dressed in the language of grievance.

He turned to Zubaida with pleading eyes and said that someone needed to make Maryam understand — that a wife was supposed to preserve her marriage, to respect her elders, to build her home rather than tear it down. That he had come here with love, with every intention of reconciling, and had been handed paperwork in return. Surely she could see how wrong this was. Surely she would speak to her daughter.

Mrs. Zubaida listened to all of it.

She had sat in that room and heard her daughter's pain, piece by piece, in the careful way Maryam had finally shared it — not dramatically, not seeking sympathy, but with the quiet precision of someone presenting evidence. She knew what her daughter had endured. She knew the surgeries performed on no sleep, the homecoming met with cold contempt, the mother dragged repeatedly into arguments as a weapon. She knew the shape of a marriage in which one person had given everything and been handed, in return, the suggestion that she was never quite enough.

She also knew something about the particular power of doing the unexpected.

"You're right, Adeel," she said.

The room stilled.

"Maryam has not managed her home the way she should. She has failed to give your family the respect they deserve. She doesn't

live according to your wishes. I admit it — she has all the flaws you say she has."

Adeel blinked. Something shifted in his expression — confusion, then a tentative relief, the beginning of the validation he had come here looking for.

Zubaida continued, her voice heavy but unfaltering.

"Everybody has flaws. Marriage is about accepting the differences and embracing the partners with all their flaws. I am not sure what expectations you have about Maryam. But if you are so bothered about her flaws, Adeel, you should divorce her. You are a good young man. Someone far better suited to you will come into your life with ease. End this today. Move forward, and may Allah grant you the happiness you deserve. That is my sincere prayer for you."

The relief on his face collapsed instantly.

What happened next was not what anyone — except perhaps Zubaida — had fully expected. Adeel, who had walked in with the composure of a man expecting to leave with his wife, crumpled. Not metaphorically. He sank toward the floor near where she sat, his composure undone entirely, tears falling without the restraint of pride.

"Aunty, please — don't say that. I cannot live without her. I love her. I will change, I swear I will change. I will do everything she wants — just please, don't ask me to let her go."

He turned to Maryam, his hands reaching toward her, his voice stripped of everything except the rawness of a man who has finally understood what he is about to lose and has no defence left.

"Maryam, please. Come home. I'll live however you want. I'll bend to your wishes. I cannot imagine my life without you. Please."

Maryam's eyes filled.

Let no one misread those tears. They were not uncertainty. They were not the beginning of a softening, the first sign of a door reopening. They were the tears of a woman mourning something real — the love that had once been genuine, the marriage that had once held beauty, the man she had chosen and believed in and given herself to completely. She was not made of stone. She had loved him. That love had been real, and its ending cost her something.

But there is a point beyond which love alone cannot carry a relationship. There is a point at which the accumulation of what has been done and left undone, said and left unsaid, defended and abandoned — there is a point at which that accumulation becomes the truest record of who someone is in the space they share with you. And Maryam had read that record carefully, in the quiet of her prayer mat, in the honest dark of her own reflection, and she knew what it said.

She looked at him — one long, complete look, carrying everything that had been and everything that would not be — and then she stood, and she walked out of the room.

The papers remained on the table, unsigned.

But her decision was not written on paper. It had been written long before this moment, in a language far more permanent.

After a while, Mrs. Zubaida turned to Adeel. Her voice, when it came, was not unkind. It was simply finished.

"Beta. It is time for you to go."

He left. Carrying himself out of that house the way people carry things that have suddenly become too heavy — slowly, carefully, as though one wrong movement might cause everything to give way at once.

Back in his own home, Adeel became a man living inside a silence he had created.

He moved through his days mechanically — the hospital, the routines, the surface of a life continuing as lives do regardless of what has broken inside them. He said little. He ate without tasting. He lay awake running the same reel of moments through his mind with the particular cruelty of hindsight — the arguments he had escalated when he could have de-escalated, the times he had chosen his family's approval over his wife's dignity, the moments when she had looked at him waiting to be defended and he had looked away.

He understood now. That was the worst of it — the clarity that arrives only when there is nothing left to do with it. He understood that his silence at the moments that mattered most had not been neutrality. It had been a choice. And every choice has a cost, and this one had cost him everything he had not known how to value until it was gone.

Maryam, on the other side of the city, was learning a different kind of quiet.

Not the hollow quiet of loss, but the full quiet of someone returning to themselves after a long absence. She woke in the mornings in her parents' home and felt — tentatively at first, then with growing steadiness — that she was still intact. That the things that made her who she was — her faith, her capability, her warmth, her absolute refusal to become bitter — had survived everything that had been thrown at them.

She believed, with a certainty that was not naive optimism but earned faith, that Allah does not waste suffering. That what had been taken from her in one form would be returned in another, better suited to who she actually was. The failed marriage was not the end of her story. It was not even the most important chapter of it.

She turned toward her career with the focused energy of someone who has stopped dividing herself. The appointment in the United States was not an escape — it was a direction. She had always been going somewhere. Now nothing stood between her and the going.

She was not defined by what had broken. She was defined, as she had always been, by how she chose to move through it.

Adeel did not find peace in his new solitude. That had been Maryam's gift — the peace she had carried into herself through prayer and honest reckoning — and it was not transferable. What he found instead was the relentless company of his own regret.

He knew the truth now with a completeness. The campaign against Maryam had been conducted by the people he loved most, and he had not only failed to stop it — he had, in his weaker moments, participated in it. He had taken a woman of extraordinary character and subjected her to the accumulated smallness of people who felt diminished by her light. And when she had looked to him — her husband, her *qawwam*, the person who had stood before Allah and promised to protect her — he had looked away.

This was what burned. Not the loss of her, though that was real and constant. But the specific, unforgiving knowledge of the moments when he had known better and chosen easier.

He prayed. Genuinely, earnestly — not the prayers of a man going through a ritual, but the prayers of someone who has nowhere else to place the weight of what he carries. He asked Allah for forgiveness with the honesty of a person who is not yet sure he deserves it. And slowly, through that honesty, something in him began to shift — not back to who he had been, but forward into someone new. Someone who had been broken open by loss and was, carefully and with great effort, being rebuilt.

He bought a house. It was not a grand gesture designed for an audience. It was something quieter and more deliberate than that — an act of sustained attention, the kind that only means something when no one is watching. He furnished it room by room with the memory of things Maryam had once mentioned in passing — the colours she loved, the kind of light she preferred in a kitchen, the way she had once described, almost to herself, what a home should feel like. He had listened, back then, without knowing he was storing it. Now he retrieved every detail and built something from it.

Not to impress her. To show her that he had heard her, even in the seasons when he had failed to act on what he heard. That she had never been invisible to him, even when his actions had made her feel that way.

When it was ready, he went to her parents' house.

Mrs. Zubaida received him with careful guardedness. She did not turn him away. She also did not make anything easy. She had watched Maryam rebuild herself from the inside out — had seen her daughter move from grief into grace with a dignity that had made her proud in ways she had no words for — and she was not about to let carelessness dismantle that.

She allowed him to see Maryam.

They sat across from each other in a quiet room, and the silence between them linger on for sometime. Neither of them rushed to fill it.

Then Adeel stood. He crossed the room and he did something that pride would once have made impossible for him. He sank to the floor before her — not as performance, but as the most honest physical expression of what he felt — and he looked up at her with eyes that had been washed clean of everything except the truth.

"Please," he said. *"Give me one more chance. Forgive me for everything."*

He went to her parents next. He bowed his head before the man who had once been dismissed on a phone call, and before the woman who had spent a lifetime fighting so that her daughter would know her own worth. He asked for their forgiveness with the simplicity of someone who has stopped calculating how it will be received and has chosen only to mean it.

Before he left, he said, quietly and without the ornamentation of grand promises: *"If you return, everything will be the way you want it. You will have a house of your own. This time, nothing will come between us."*

Then he left her to decide.

Maryam sat with his words for a long time.

She was not the woman who had stood in a hospital corridor exhausted and come home to contempt. She was not the woman who had wept on a prayer mat wondering where her marriage had gone. She had moved through that fire and emerged as someone who no longer needed rescue.

That was the only position from which she could genuinely consider returning. Not from fear, not from loneliness, not from the social pressure that she had never once allowed to govern her decisions. But from strength, and from a choice made by a whole person rather than a diminished one.

She looked at what Adeel had done — not what he had said, but what he had *done*. The house. The months of quiet accountability. The prayer. The descent to the floor that no amount of cultural conditioning had made easy for him. She knew the distance he had traveled to arrive at that room, because she understood, better than most, how far it was from where he had started.

She also knew something that only a woman of genuine faith can know in a moment like this: that forgiveness is not weakness. That choosing to rebuild, when the rebuilding is done with full sight and clear terms, is not a retreat from the strength she had found — it is the fullest expression of it.

She made her decision — in prayer, in honesty, and entirely on her own terms.

This is where their story turns.

Not into a fairy tale — real life is never that, and Maryam had always been too clear-eyed for fairy tales. But into something more durable than a fairy tale: a second beginning, entered into with the full knowledge of what the first one had cost, and therefore with a seriousness and gratitude that first beginnings rarely carry.

Adeel became, in time, the man he had always had the capacity to be. Not perfect — he would be the first to say so — but present. Accountable. The kind of husband who had learned, through the worst possible teacher, that love is not a feeling you receive but a practice you choose, daily, in the small decisions no one else sees. He let go of the ego that had made him easy to manipulate and hard to live with. He chose Maryam — consistently, visibly, without requiring his family's approval to do so.

And in doing so, he found that he had not only saved his marriage. He had saved himself.

In today's times, when divorce is often seen as a simple and common solution to marital problems, their story stood out. Divorce itself is not shocking anymore; what is remarkable, however, is when two people choose to learn from past mistakes, forgive each other, and rebuild their relationship with maturity. That requires far greater strength than simply walking away.

Both men and women must understand that if one is fortunate enough to find a good life partner, it is essential to recognize their worth and cherish them. Love and compatibility are rare blessings, and they should not be taken for granted. Otherwise, regret becomes the only companion left when the relationship is gone.

Their journey shows that relationships demand effort, patience, and the humility to accept one's faults. True strength lies not in never faltering but in rising after mistakes and striving to do better. Maryam and Adeel became examples of how resilience, forgiveness, and mutual respect can turn even broken bonds into stronger, more beautiful ones.

* * * * *

Chapter 3

Shabnam – The Story of Self Restraint

She came into the world with nothing — and the world, it seemed, was in no hurry to give her anything.

Shabnam was the youngest of five children, born to a father who carried the weight of the entire household on a labourer's wages. Every morning he left before the sun was properly up, trading his body for whatever the day would pay him. It was rarely enough. Two meals a day was not a given in that house — it was an achievement, celebrated quietly and without complaint.

From the very beginning, life was stingy with Shabnam. Milk was a luxury. Proper food was a negotiation. She grew up thin and pale, her small body carrying the quiet damage of malnutrition before she was old enough to understand what that word meant. And then, when she was barely a year old, her mother died.

In a neighbourhood where people scraped to eat, medicine was a distant dream. Illness came, and it took what it wanted. After her mother was gone, her grandmother stepped forward — an old woman with tired bones and a determined heart — and held the family together as best she could. She cooked, she watched, she worried. But five young children are a tide that even the most loving grandmother cannot fully hold back.

Then came Khalida.

Shabnam's father remarried, and with his new wife came new children — two daughters and a son — and the already stretched household grew tighter still. To ease the financial pressure, the elder boys were pulled out of whatever chance at childhood they had and sent to work. They brought home small wages and lost large futures, and nobody seemed to think this was worth grieving.

Khalida was, in every sense, the stepmother from every story you were ever warned about. She wore her bitterness openly and without shame. The money Shabnam's brothers earned passed through their hands and into hers. Shabnam's elder sisters were turned into house servants — cleaning, cooking, scrubbing — while Khalida's own children were dressed neatly and sent off to school each morning. When food was served, the fresh portions went to her children. What remained — stale, sometimes spoiled — was left for Shabnam and her siblings. The message was never spoken aloud. It didn't need to be. Children understand cruelty without being told.

Years passed, and Shabnam grew without ever once receiving a new dress. She wore what was old, what was worn, what nobody else wanted. The neglect settled into her skin like cold weather — permanent, unannounced, always there.

But Shabnam endured. Quietly, stubbornly, in the way that children do when they have no other choice.

Her elder sisters, when they were old enough, married men who were decent and hardworking — men who offered them a way out. Khalida fought those marriages with everything she had. She argued with Shabnam's father, told him his daughters deserved nothing, that they should stay and serve. But for once, she did not get her way. Both sisters left, and their lives opened up into something kinder.

Khalida's fury, now with nowhere else to go, landed squarely on eight-year-old Shabnam.

Every chore in the house became hers. Dishes. Laundry. Floors. By twelve, she was cooking full meals for the entire family — her small hands managing pots and flames that were too heavy for her age. When something delicious was prepared, Khalida and her children ate at the table while Shabnam watched, hungry and invisible. Her brothers, older now and earning, had drifted into a different kind of lost — bad company, bad habits, money spent on various addiction and of course no sense of responsibility towards their younger sister. Her father had chosen Khalida completely. His fear of upsetting his wife was stronger than any instinct to protect his child.

The only soft place in Shabnam's life was her grandmother.

It was her grandmother who made sure Shabnam could attend the local madrasa each afternoon — just an hour and a half, sometimes two hours, carved out of the harshness of her days. The Qari sahib there taught for free, asking nothing from children who had nothing to give. And in that small, simple room, something in Shabnam came alive.

She learned to read the Qur'an. She learned her prayers. She fasted. She sat and listened to the stories of the Prophets — their patience, their trials, their unshakeable trust in Allah — and something in those stories recognised her, or she recognised herself in them. The words of the Prophet ﷺ reached her in a language her heart already knew. For those few hours each day, the world became bearable. Gentle, even.

Then her grandmother died, and the gentleness went with her.

Her brothers had their own homes now. Her sisters had long since moved on. Shabnam was alone in a house that had never truly wanted her, with no one left to soften the edges of Khalida's cruelty. And when Shabnam turned fourteen, even the madrasa was taken from her. Khalida decided she could no longer be spared for that small mercy, and so it ended.

The door closed. The last light went out.

Shabnam's world shrank to four walls, endless chores, and a stepmother whose anger needed no reason. Any mistake — sometimes no mistake at all — was enough to bring Khalida's hand down on her. Shabnam learned to move quietly through the house, to take up as little space as possible, to make herself small enough to be overlooked.

But small and broken are not the same thing. And Shabnam, though she did not yet know it, was far from broken.

By the time Shabnam turned sixteen, Khalida had one last cruelty left to offer her — a husband.

Not a good one. Not even a passable one. Khalida chose deliberately, the way someone picks a punishment. The young man's name was Asim, and he was known in the community the way certain people are known — not for anything worth admiring. He did not work. He did not intend to. His days were spent in idleness, his evenings clouded with alcohol and ganja, his presence on the roadside the kind that made decent people cross the street. He had no trade, no ambition, no particular plan for his life beyond getting through it with the least effort possible.

Khalida knew all of this. That was precisely why she chose him.

Shabnam's father, as he had always done, said nothing. His silence had long since stopped being a surprise. He arranged the wedding as his wife instructed, borrowed what money he could, and told himself he had done what a father does. Shabnam, who had spent her entire childhood watching her sisters' marriages lift them into better lives, allowed herself — just this once — to hope. She imagined new clothes, a home of her own, the simple dignity of being someone's wife rather than someone's servant. She had asked so little of life. Surely life could manage this much.

It could not.

On the night of her wedding, Asim came to her drunk.

He did not come with warmth or nervousness or the awkward tenderness of a new husband. He came with anger. He slapped her. He screamed at her family for failing to provide a motorcycle — his friends had all received motorcycles, he told her, as if this were her fault, as if she had personally wronged him by arriving without one. He told her, coldly and clearly, not to expect anything from him. And then the night ended, and Shabnam sat alone with the wreckage of every hope she had quietly carried into that room.

In the span of a few hours, sixteen years of endurance had led her here.

Within a week, the shape of her new life had made itself plain. The chores she had performed at her father's house — the cooking, the cleaning, the endless invisible labour — simply transferred to her in-laws' home. Same work. Colder walls. Her husband's hands found her whenever his mood soured, which was often. Her in-laws watched and saw nothing wrong. In that household, a daughter-in-law's suffering was not a problem to be solved — it was simply the order of things, as natural and unremarkable as the weather.

The dreams dissolved. What remained was survival.

Years passed in this way. Shabnam gave birth to two daughters — Zahra and Zeba — and poured into them whatever tenderness she could still find in herself. But the body keeps its own accounts. The poor food, the relentless work, the beatings that came without warning or reason — all of it had worn her down until she was thin as paper, fragile in a way that went far deeper than the physical. She rose at dawn and did not stop until long after dark. And somewhere in between, she made sure her daughters were fed.

She was not alone in her suffering, though that brought no comfort.

The village was full of women like her — young brides who had arrived with hope and found themselves, within months, absorbed into a life of labour and silence. Most accepted it the way you accept rain — because it comes regardless, and there is no point in argument. But some did not accept it. Some found other ways.

Whispers moved through the narrow lanes the way whispers always do — half-heard, quickly buried, but never entirely gone. Women were seeking elsewhere what their marriages had never given them. Affection. The feeling of being chosen. Affairs, secret and not-so-secret, had become woven quietly into the fabric of village life. Some women left altogether — disappearing with men from the village, married or otherwise — and the scandal would flare for a week before fading into the next piece of gossip. For these women, it was not simply about passion. It was about feeling alive. About existing as more than a pair of hands that cooked and cleaned and absorbed punishment.

Even women who had been married for years, with children old enough to understand, walked this road. The weight had simply become too much. And so they chose escape over duty, desire over consequence, the present moment over everything they were supposed to protect.

Shabnam watched all of this. She understood it — the desperation underneath, the hunger for something that felt like dignity. She did not judge those women as harshly as the village did. She knew what drove them to it.

But she also saw what it cost. The lies that had to be maintained, day after day, each one built on the last. The way the children were quietly abandoned to the edges of their mothers' attention. The person you had to become to keep it all hidden — harder, more dishonest, more hollow — until one morning you woke up and could not find yourself at all. The road began as an escape and ended somewhere much darker, somewhere you could not easily come back from.

Shabnam looked at that road and turned away.

She was different — not because her pain was smaller, or because she was made of stronger material than the women around her. She was different because somewhere inside her, in a place that years of cruelty had not managed to reach, something had taken root. Something quiet. Something that held.

Every night, without fail, she prayed.

It didn't matter how exhausted she was, how bruised, how hollowed out by the day. When the last chore was done and the house had finally gone quiet, Shabnam would spread her prayer mat and fold herself into Isha. Those few minutes were hers — truly, completely hers — in a way that nothing else in her life was. She would place her forehead on the mat and speak to Allah the way you speak to someone who is actually listening. She told Him everything. The fear she swallowed every morning. The grief she carried for her daughters. The weariness that had settled so deep into her bones she wasn't sure it would ever leave.

And somehow, she would rise from that mat a little lighter than she had gone down.

People who watched Shabnam from the outside might have mistaken her quietness for resignation — for the blank acceptance of a woman who had stopped expecting better. In some ways, perhaps, she had grown numb. The beatings, the insults, the daily grind of a life that gave nothing back — she had learned to absorb these things the way the earth absorbs rain. Without theatre. Without collapse. She kept moving, because her daughters needed her to keep moving.

Zahra had turned four. Little Zeba was barely a year old.

Each morning, Shabnam would watch the village children file past — school bags on their backs, shoes raising small clouds of dust, voices tumbling over each other with the careless noise of children who had nowhere urgent to be. She watched them the way a person watches something they want so badly the wanting becomes a kind of ache. She did not want this for herself anymore. She had given up on herself years ago, without quite realising it. But for Zahra and Zeba — for them, the wanting was fierce and clean and utterly non-negotiable.

She tried to talk to Asim about enrolling Zahra in school.

Again and again, she tried.

Each time, she got the same answer, delivered with the same contemptuous ease: *What's the use of educating girls? They'll either run off with someone or end up exactly like you — doing housework after marriage.* The words hit her somewhere precise and specific, like he knew exactly where to aim. Her daughters' futures, dismissed in a single breath. Reduced to punchlines.

Something changed in Shabnam after those conversations.

The woman who had swallowed a lifetime of humiliation, to her own surprise, that she could not swallow this. She began to argue back. It cost her — it always cost her — but she paid the price without flinching. The beatings she could bear. What she could not bear was silence in the face of her children being told they were worth nothing. The same Shabnam who had never once raised her voice for herself was now unmovable when it came to her daughters. Asim's violence had extinguished many things in her over the years. It could not extinguish this.

Then, as if in answer to all those nights on the prayer mat, a door opened.

Asim was offered work as a labourer in Delhi — six months, steady wages. He decided to take Shabnam and the girls with him. They arrived in the city and settled into a single cramped room near the boundary wall of a large residential society. For Shabnam, it was enough. More than enough. It was somewhere else.

Asim left early each morning and returned late, and in the hours between, something quietly extraordinary happened: Shabnam began to breathe.

She made friends with the women in the settlement — mostly house helps employed in the society nearby — and before long, she joined them. She cleaned homes, she worked hard, she smiled at the families who thanked her. And at the end of the month, she received her first salary.

Five thousand rupees.

She stood holding the notes and felt something she did not have a word for. She had worked her entire life — since childhood, really — but her labour had always disappeared into someone else's household, someone else's benefit, without a rupee or a word of thanks to mark that she had been there at all. This was different. This money existed because of *her*. Her hands, her effort, her early mornings. For the first time in her life, her work had been seen and rewarded.

No amount of money given freely could have felt like this.

That same afternoon, she took Zahra and Zeba to the market.

She bought them new clothes — proper new clothes, not someone else's leftovers. She let them choose their favourite foods. And then, almost shyly, she bought them toys. Little plastic things, bright colours, nothing expensive — but the girls held them as if they were made of something precious, and perhaps they were. Shabnam watched her daughters' faces and felt the specific joy of a person who has earned the right to give.

They piled into an auto-rickshaw for the ride home, the girls pressed close against her, warm and drowsy and content.

Then Zahra looked up at her — four years old, eyes still shining — and said, very simply: *"Amma, will you also buy me a school bag?"*

Shabnam went still.

She had spent years wishing this for her daughter. Years of fighting and praying and enduring Asim's contempt on the subject. But hearing it from Zahra herself — hearing her daughter *ask* for it, want it, reach for it with her own small hands — was something else entirely. The wish had always been Shabnam's. Now, suddenly, it belonged to both of them.

The auto rattled on through the city streets. Both girls fell asleep in her lap, their breathing slow and even, their new toys still clutched in their fingers. Thirty minutes. Shabnam sat awake in the dark with her daughters' weight against her and made the most important decisions of her life.

She would not go back to the village.

She would stay in Delhi. She would work. She would send Zahra and Zeba to school — real school — and she would keep them there. She would raise them to be capable, self-reliant, free in a way she herself had never been. The five thousand rupees in her bag had shown her something she could not unsee: that her hands had value, that her effort had worth, that a different life was not a fantasy dreamed up on a prayer mat — it was something that could be *built*.

She had tasted independence for the first time at twenty-something years old, in the back of an auto-rickshaw, with her daughters asleep on her lap.

It tasted like a beginning.

Asim had not changed. Delhi had not changed him, new surroundings had not changed him, fatherhood had not changed him. He was the same man he had always been — idle, drinking, burning through whatever little they had, filling the room with a particular kind of misery that only the chronically self-destructive can generate. He skipped work. He came home smelling of liquor and looking for a reason to be angry. Barely two and a half months after they had arrived, he began pushing to go back to the village.

This time, Shabnam did not bend.

Something had shifted in her — quietly, irreversibly — and she could feel it in the steadiness of her own hands. She knew what going back meant. It meant surrendering the only glimpse of hope she had ever been given. It meant returning her daughters to the same dusty lanes, the same closed horizons, the same life she had been trying to outrun since she was eight years old with a broom in her hands. She would accept hardship — she had never known anything else — but she would only accept it now on her own terms, in service of something worth fighting for.

She looked at Zahra and Zeba as they slept and let the decision settle into her, clean and final.

Asim was not her husband in any meaningful sense of the word. He was a weight around her neck, and she had been drowning in small increments for years. There was a word in her faith— *khula* — a woman's right to walk out of a marital relationship. She had turned it over in her mind many times before, always pulling back. Not out of any love for him, but out of the God-consciousness that had been her anchor since those afternoons at the madrasa, the deep awareness that she was bound by a sacred contract, that her dignity before Allah mattered more than her comfort, that patience was its own form of prayer.

But she understood something now that she had not understood before.

Enduring cruelty in silence is not always piety. Sometimes, choosing yourself — choosing your children — with a clean heart and sincere intention is the higher form of courage. She had not once, in all her years of suffering, allowed her eyes or her heart to drift toward anything forbidden. Not a glance, not a thought she was ashamed of. Her fear of Allah had kept her straight even when her life gave her every reason to go crooked. And it was that same fear, now transformed into something warmer and steadier — *trust* — that was showing her the way forward.

Allah does not abandon the sincere. She had heard this said at the madrasa when she was a girl. She believed it then because she was told to. She believed it now because she had lived long enough to understand what it meant.

She was nearly home, her daughters' hands in hers, when she walked through the door and found Asim waiting.

He had been waiting for her salary. That was the truth of it — he had not been thinking about his daughters or his wife or the shopping bags in Shabnam's hands. He had been calculating what she owed him, what he could take, what would cover his debts and keep his glass full. When he understood that she had already spent part of the money — on *toys*, on *clothes*, on the children — something in him ignited.

He rose from where he was sitting and hit her.

Not once. The sounds filled the small room and spilled out through the thin walls into the settlement beyond, where two women heard them and did not look away.

Soni and Leelawati had become Shabnam's friends in the way that neighbours become friends when they share close walls and honest conversation — they knew her, they knew her story, they had seen the bruises she never quite explained. They had watched Asim before. But that evening, something crossed a line that neither of them could accept in silence. They came — and they brought their husbands with them.

The men pulled Asim off her. What followed was swift and without mercy: Asim received back some measure of what he had been freely distributing for years, and in the confrontation, his leg broke. Soni and Leelawati, standing straight with the particular fury of women who have had enough, went to the police and filed an FIR.

Asim was arrested. He was taken away, and the room went quiet in a way it had never been quiet before.

Shabnam sat in that silence and tried to understand what had just happened. People say that help comes from Allah in ways the mind cannot always trace — that sometimes you cannot tell where your prayers end and your destiny begins, where coincidence stops and grace starts. She had been beaten her whole life and her blood relatives had watched without moving, had classified her suffering as a domestic matter, too ordinary to intervene in. Her own family had looked at her bruises and looked away. But two women who had known her for less than three months had walked through a door and changed everything.

Perhaps that was the answer to all those nights on the prayer mat. Delivered in unusual but practical way and with great timing.

The fear that had lived in her chest for as long as she could remember — that low, constant hum of *what will he do today* — was gone. In its place there was quite in the room.

And in that quiet, for the first time, she could hear herself think.

There is a particular kind of damage that comes not from a single blow but from years of accumulated ones — the kind that doesn't leave visible bruises but quietly hollows a person out from the inside. By the time Asim was taken away, Shabnam had been so thoroughly worn down by suffering that she had, without realising it, begun to forget herself. Not her name, not her face, but the deeper thing — that she was a human being, that she was, in the eyes of her Creator, something precious. That knowledge had been ground down to almost nothing.

Three months after Asim's arrest, with the help of the city qazi, Shabnam's divorce was finalised. She walked out of that process not broken, as many had perhaps expected, but upright. Beside her, as they had been for every difficult step of those months — the courts, the paperwork, the sideways glances of the society— were Soni and Leelawati.

They had become, in the truest sense, her sisters.

Not in the way the word is used carelessly. In the way that actually means something — the kind of sisterhood that shows up at the worst moments, that doesn't flinch from inconvenience, that sits with you in courtrooms and shields you from whispers and says, without needing to say it aloud, *I see you, and you are not alone.* They never once let the differences between them — in faith, in background, in the language of their prayers — become a reason to step back. They placed humanity above every category the world uses to divide people, and in doing so, they gave Shabnam something her own blood relatives had withheld her entire life: the simple, radical experience of being stood up for.

Shabnam understood, with a clarity that settled in her chest like warm light, that this was how Allah answers prayers. Not always in the form you expect. Not always through the people you think will come. Sometimes He sends help wearing the face of a neighbour you've known for three months, and you only recognise it as divine mercy afterwards, when you sit quietly and trace back the thread of how you survived.

She enrolled Zahra and Zeba in school from next session.

The years that followed were not without difficulty. New problems arrived, as they always do — money was tight, the city was demanding, raising two daughters alone required a constant juggling of energy and worry and love. But Shabnam had developed, over a lifetime of hardship, a kind of spiritual musculature that most people never need to build. Each time something threatened to knock her down, she returned to what she had always returned to: the prayer mat, the quiet conversation with her Lord, the unshakeable conviction that she was held.

And her daughters grew.

Zahra and Zeba absorbed their mother without being told to. They watched how she moved through the world — with honesty, with dignity, without bitterness, without ever allowing her tongue to form a lie or her heart to wish harm on another person — and they became it. The values Shabnam had carried from that small madrasa classroom, through years of abuse and poverty and survival, passed into her daughters as naturally as a mother tongue. When their education was complete, their characters were already formed — confident, principled, and kind.

Zahra became a makeup artist at a respected salon — skilled, sought-after, bringing joy to her work. Zeba went into healthcare, working in a pathology lab, quiet and precise and devoted to her work completely. Both sisters built lives that were entirely their own — independent, dignified, and rooted in the values their mother had fought to give them.

In time, they both married well. Kind men. Good families. Homes where they were treated with respect.

Shabnam sat at those weddings and felt something she could not have imagined feeling on her own wedding night, all those years ago. She felt *proud.* Not the brittle pride of someone who needs to show the world they've won. The quiet, deep, almost wordless pride of a mother who kept her promise to her children.

She was fifty-two now.

She worked at an NGO, cooking meals for children who needed them — a detail that, if you knew her story, contained a kind of poetry. The girl who had once been deliberately given stale food while others ate fresh, who had gone years without a new dress, who had cooked for a household that treated her like furniture — that same woman now fed children every day, and she did it with care and with joy. She had built herself a small home: one room, a hall, walls that held no memory of violence. Her grandchildren visited and filled it with noise and laughter, and she let it wash over her like something she had earned, because she had.

She earned her living through halal means, through her own two hands, with her head held straight. She had raised daughters who made her proud not just in their careers but in their characters. She had a roof that was hers. She had peace.

What more, she thought, could a faithful heart ask for?

Chapter 4

Jacob and Yusuf – Friends Forever

Thomas had decided, with the quiet certainty of a man who has made up his mind and is simply waiting for the right moment, that he wanted to marry Amelia.

Three years they had lived together in their flat in the UK — three years of morning coffee and shared routines and the comfort of knowing another person's habits by heart. He loved her. That part was simple. The rest, he was beginning to discover, was considerably more complicated.

Amelia did not believe in marriage.

Not in a casual, vague sort of way — she had genuinely thought it through and arrived at a conclusion. Whenever she found herself near a married couple, especially one with children, something in her visibly deflated. She would watch them — the nappy bags, the negotiated schedules, the conversations interrupted every forty seconds by a small demanding person — and she simply could not understand the appeal. Why, she wondered, would anyone willingly choose this? Why trade spontaneity for routine, freedom for obligation. Surely life was for *living* — new places, new people, new experiences — not for slowly disappearing into someone else's domestic arrangements.

Thomas knew all of this. He had heard her views many times, delivered with the confidence of someone who has not yet been asked to revise them. He never argued. He would smile, maybe laugh a little, and privately overlooked her opinions thinking *she'll feel differently about when she's ready.* He loved her too much to take her seriously on this particular point. People grew, he told himself. Amelia would grow.

He proposed on an ordinary evening, in the way that people do when they've been rehearsing it in their heads and finally decide the waiting is worse than the asking.

Amelia's face did something he hadn't anticipated. It went blank.

Not cold — not cruel — just genuinely, openly uncertain, like a person who has walked into a room and forgotten why they came. She had always known Thomas wanted this. She had known it for years, in the background of everything, the way you know a bill is coming without looking at the calendar. But knowing it abstractly and being asked directly were, she discovered in that moment, two entirely different things.

She loved being with Thomas. She did not want to lose him. She also did not want a lifetime of responsibility handed to her in a velvet box. Both of these things were equally true, pulling at her from opposite directions with equal force.

She asked for time.

Thomas gave it to her — generously, without complaint, because that is the kind of man he was.

A few days passed, and Amelia said yes.

Thomas's heart lifted immediately, completely, without stopping to ask questions. His girlfriend was going to be his wife. That was all that mattered. He was financially stable, his business was growing, the future looked spacious and good, and now Amelia had said yes. What more was there to examine?

He did not think too carefully about what had actually changed her mind, which was perhaps his first mistake — not because he was foolish, but because he was in love, and love has a way of making you focus on the answer rather than the reasoning behind it.

What had changed Amelia's mind was this: a wedding.

Not the marriage exactly — the wedding. The photographs, the gown, the moment of being the most looked-at person in a room, the Instagram posts that would follow, the comments and the likes and the particular glow of being admired by people you barely knew. She had run the numbers in her head, quietly and without guilt, and concluded that the attention would be worth it. People would talk about her. They would praise the dress. They would save the photos. She would exist, for a brief and glittering moment, at the very centre of everyone's attention.

That was enough. She said yes.

The wedding was everything she had imagined — grand, photographed beautifully, celebrated loudly. Her social media notifications ran for days. The comments were exactly as she had hoped. She read each one with quiet satisfaction.

Thomas bought them a house soon after — large, modern, full of light, with a garden that stretched generously behind it. Amelia walked through the rooms and was pleased. Life, she told herself, was good. The first year passed without serious incident, the way first years often do, carried along by novelty and the residual warmth of the wedding.

But marriage, by its very nature, is not a photograph. It is not a moment you can frame and caption and move on from. It is built from commitment — and commitment, unlike a like or a comment, requires something of you every single day.

Amelia had always found this part of the arrangement quietly unreasonable, and marriage, it turned out, had not changed that.

Thomas, meanwhile, had begun to think about children.

He thought about it the way people think about something they've always wanted — not frantically, not obsessively, but with a warm and steady longing that was simply part of who he was. He adored children. He wanted a family, a home that was full in the way homes are full when small people live in them. To Thomas, having children was not a sacrifice or a compromise. It was the whole point.

One evening, with all the tenderness he had, he told Amelia this.

She stared at him as though he had suggested something genuinely unhinged.

"Are you out of your mind?" Her voice went up in a way that left no ambiguity about how she felt. *"You know I have absolutely no interest in children. I can't imagine ruining my figure or taking on a responsibility like that for the rest of my life."*

The words landed on Thomas with a particular kind of weight — not just the sting of rejection, but the dawning awareness that the woman he had married and the woman he had imagined he was marrying were, on this matter at least, two very different people.

The arguments that followed lasted days. The same ground, covered again and again. Amelia, immovable. Thomas, increasingly unable to understand how two people who loved each other had arrived at such a fundamental impasse.

The gap between them had always been there. They were only now beginning to see how wide it was.

Amelia had, without making any formal announcement, already begun considering divorce.

She turned the idea over in her mind the way you turn over a stone — carefully, checking what lives underneath. She was thirty-five. She was beautiful. She had, she felt, a great deal of life still ahead of her that did not yet involve being permanently attached to one person and the accumulated weight of his expectations. The world was large and she had seen only a fraction of it. New places, new experiences, the clean exhilaration of living entirely on your own terms — these were the things that called to her. Children, in this vision, did not appear. They were not part of the landscape. They were, if she was honest with herself, the thing that would ruin it.

Thomas knew none of this. Or perhaps he knew and chose not to look directly at it, the way you avoid looking at something that would require you to act if you saw it clearly.

He loved her. That remained uncomplicated and constant, even now, even after the arguments, even after her words had landed on him with that particular sharpness. He had married Amelia knowing who she was, and he was not the kind of man who loved conditionally or kept a running account of disappointments. But he was also a man with a longing he could not reason away — and that longing had a shape now, clear and specific. He wanted a child. He wanted to be a father. He had wanted it long before he could admit it out loud, and every visit to a colleague's home, every friend's baby held briefly in his arms, had only sharpened the wanting.

He could not make Amelia want the same thing. But perhaps, he thought, there was another way.

Surrogacy. He contemplated the idea carefully and thoroughly. In today's world it was not unusual — people built families through many different routes, and this one had a particular logic to it. Amelia would not have to carry a child. Her body, her figure, her freedom of movement — none of it would be touched. And yet there could still be a family. A child in the house. A future that felt, to Thomas, like the whole point of everything he had been building.

He knew better than to raise it immediately. He gave it weeks — weeks of quiet effort, of being present and patient and affectionate, of letting the temperature between them settle. He was, in this way, a careful and loving man. When he finally chose his moment, they were on holiday, somewhere calm and unhurried, the kind of place where conversations feel less dangerous.

One evening, relaxed and close, he said it gently. Surrogacy. No pregnancy for her. A child for them. A family, in whatever form she could accept.

Amelia listened. She was quiet for a moment in a way that Thomas read, hopefully, as consideration.

Then she said: *"If you want a child, go ahead. I won't stop you. But the child will be yours, not mine. I won't contribute my eggs. I don't want to be a mother. But yes — we can still live together."*

Thomas sat with this answer for a long moment.

It was not a no. He held onto that. After everything, after all the arguments and the hard words and the growing silence on this subject, she had not said no. He was grateful for this — genuinely, immediately grateful — in the way that people who love deeply are sometimes grateful for far less than they deserve. But underneath the gratitude, something quieter troubled him. A family, as he understood it, was not a legal arrangement or a shared address. It was love distributed equally, responsibility held together, a child who belonged to both parents in the full sense of the word. What Amelia was describing was something else. Something he didn't quite have a name for.

He told himself her feelings might change once the child was real. Once she held him. Once she knew him.

He chose to believe this because the alternative — that she meant exactly what she said — was something he could not yet afford to look at.

He contacted an agency. They were professional, discreet, thorough — they handled everything and kept the surrogate's details entirely confidential, which suited Thomas fine. He signed the paperwork with the careful attention of a man who has waited a long time for something and does not want to get it wrong. Then he waited.

A year later, Jacob arrived.

He was beautiful in the way that newborns are beautiful — small and new and startlingly real, in a way that no amount of anticipation quite prepares you for. Thomas held his son and felt something settle into place inside him that had been restless for years. He had already arranged a babysitter before the birth, practical and prepared as always, making sure Jacob would be properly looked after.

Amelia looked at Jacob with the expression of someone who has agreed to something and is now confronted with its full reality. She was not unkind. She was not cruel. She was simply absent from it all in the way she had warned Thomas she would be — present in the house, present at the edges, but not *there* in the way that Jacob needed someone to be there.

In the first five months of his life, Amelia did not once prepare his bottle.

The maid did it. The babysitter did it. The small, ordinary act of feeding an infant — the most basic form of closeness available to a person who is not nursing — simply did not happen between Amelia and Jacob. Not once.

Thomas came home each evening after long days and went directly to his son. The time was short — an hour, sometimes less — but he was *present* in it, fully and deliberately, in the way of a man who understands that showing up consistently is its own form of love. He had named him Jacob. He said the name with a quiet pride every time.

The house was large and well-appointed and full of every comfort money could provide.

And Jacob, five months old, lay in it — fed by hired hands, loved fiercely by one parent, and existing, for the other, somewhere at the outer edge of a life she had not entirely agreed to share.

Jacob turned six months old, and the world noticed him before his own so called mother did.

He had become, somewhere in those early weeks, extraordinarily cherubic and beautiful - Round-cheeked, bright-eyed, with a laugh that arrived easily and often. The kind of baby that strangers feel compelled to comment on, that neighbours ask to hold, that fills a room with a particular warmth simply by being in it. He smiled at everyone. He had not yet learned to be cautious about people.

Amelia noticed the smiles. She noticed, more precisely, what they did to other people — the way guests leaned toward Jacob, the way the atmosphere in any room shifted when he laughed. She had an instinct for attention, an awareness of where it gathered and why. And Jacob, she began to understand, was extraordinary at gathering it.

She introduced him on Instagram.

The posts were beautiful — the image of a happy young mother and her cherubic son. The comments came quickly and in volume. People who had stopped following her returned. New followers arrived. The numbers that had quietly been declining reversed themselves, climbing steadily back toward where she wanted them. Jacob's chubby face, his genuine unperformable delight in being alive — these were, it turned out, exactly what her audience had been waiting for.

Amelia had found, without quite planning it, her best content.

Meanwhile, Thomas was doing something quieter and less photogenic. He was coming home every evening and sitting with his son. An hour, sometimes less — whatever the day had left him — but he was *there* in it, fully, talking to Jacob in the soft deliberate way you talk to someone you are trying to know. He was building something real, in small increments, with whatever time he had.

Three years passed in this way. Jacob grew from an infant into a small boy — talking now, curious, still possessed of that easy warmth that had characterised him from the beginning. But Amelia had grown restless in a way that the house could no longer contain.

Eight or nine years, counting everything. The live-in arrangement, the wedding, the house, Jacob's arrival — all of it added up to nearly a decade of shared life. And Amelia, at the end of it, felt what she had perhaps always been prone to feeling: that this was no longer new, that the edges of her life here had become familiar. She wanted change. She wanted the sensation of a door opening rather than the reality of one already walked through.

Thomas had felt it coming. He was an observant man, and Amelia had never been particularly difficult to read — not because she was transparent, but because she had never pretended to want things she didn't want.

When she told him she wanted a divorce, he did not collapse. He did not argue, or plead, or do any of the things his love for her might have entitled him to do. He helped her leave with the same quiet generosity that had characterised everything he had ever done for her. The paperwork was completed without drama. He said goodbye with dignity, and if his heart was breaking underneath it, he kept that private.

Amelia walked out of a peaceful home, a comfortable life, and a partner who had loved her faithfully for nearly a decade. She left in pursuit of something she could not name precisely but felt certain was waiting for her somewhere else.

She did not look back.

And Jacob — three years old, just beginning to understand the shape of the world around him — watched the woman who had called herself his mother on the internet disappear from his daily life, and said nothing, because he did not yet have the words for what he was losing.

Thomas told himself the transition would be manageable. Jacob was already accustomed to the nanny, to the rotation of caregivers who had always been the reliable centre of his daily routine. A mother's absence, Thomas reasoned, would not create a gap that was not already there. Life would continue as it had.

He was wrong, and it took a birthday party to show him.

A friend's child was turning five — a cheerful, crowded afternoon of cake and noise and small people running in every direction. Thomas brought Jacob, partly for the social occasion and partly, if he was honest, out of a vague guilt that his son did not spend enough time around other children.

He watched Jacob from across the room.

The boy who had once walked into any gathering and immediately begun talking — asking questions, making friends, filling the space around him with that easy unguarded warmth — was standing against the wall. Not playing. Not watching with curiosity. Just standing, still, his small shoulders pulled inward, his face carrying an expression that did not belong on a three-year-old: a careful, watchful fear, as though the room contained something he needed to be ready for.

Other children ran past him. He did not join them. A couple of them called to him. He didn't respond. He retreated further into the corner, as if hoping to take up less space, to be less visible, to need less from a world that had already shown him it was not entirely reliable.

Thomas felt something tighten in his chest.

He crossed the room and crouched beside his son, and then — because he was tired and guilty and did not know what else to do with either of those feelings — he said the wrong thing. *"Look at the other children. They're all having fun. I brought you here to enjoy yourself, not to sit in a corner."* His voice came out with an edge he hadn't intended.

Jacob's eyes filled immediately.

He didn't argue. He didn't explain himself. He simply went quieter, smaller, further away — and the sight of his son's lip trembling, of those careful eyes now spilling over, hit Thomas somewhere deep and precise, like a key turning in a lock he hadn't known was there.

He straightened up and looked around at the party — at the other children and their noise and their unselfconscious joy — and then back at his son pressed against the wall, trying not to cry in front of strangers.

And Thomas understood, with a clarity that was almost physical, what he had done.

Not just today, not just the scolding — but all of it. The choices that had seemed reasonable at the time, the compromises he had made with himself, the things he had told himself Jacob would not notice or would grow out of or would be adequately compensated for by nannies and stability and a large comfortable house. He had brought a child into a home that was already running on borrowed warmth, already patched together with arrangements rather than devotion, and he had told himself it was enough.

The cheerful, curious, fearlessly sociable little boy that Jacob had been was retreating. Slowly, incrementally, in the way that children retreat when the world stops feeling safe.

Jacob had never known his mother's arms. He had known the arms of whoever was on shift that week. And his father, who loved him genuinely and deeply, had been available for a fraction of each day — an hour in the evenings, well-intentioned and real, but not enough. Not nearly enough.

Thomas stood at that birthday party with guilt settled on him like weather, and the question that had been quietly waiting for him finally arrived, unavoidable:

What had he done to his son?

Thomas's business did not slow down to accommodate his guilt.

If anything, it accelerated — new markets, new partnerships, a diary that filled itself faster than he could empty it. Travel became a constant. Meetings extending till late evenings. The hour he had once protected for Jacob each day became harder to guarantee. He told himself that stability required sacrifice, that providing well for Jacob was itself a form of love, that a permanent nanny and a reliable maid were the practical solution a responsible father arranges when his circumstances demand it.

He hired two experienced permanent nanny and maid available now 24x7 around Thomas.

What he did not know — could not know, because Jacob had no language yet for what was being done to him and no adult nearby to tell — was that the two women had, quite quickly, understood the situation for what it was. The father was away most of the time. The child had no one to run to. There was no one watching.

Things went on OK for some time, but later on nanny started taking her frustrations out on Jacob. The maid moved through the house as though she owned it, dismissing Jacob's needs with the ease of someone who has correctly identified that there will be no consequences. Together, they had created, inside that bright and well-appointed home, a private world of fear that Jacob woke up to every morning and went to sleep inside every night.

He had stopped being chatty. He had stopped asking questions. He was four years old and he had already learned that drawing attention to yourself was dangerous.

Then one afternoon, when Thomas was on an international trip, in the garden, it went further than it had ever gone before.

The nanny's temper broke completely. She hit Jacob — not once, not the sharp reflexive smack of someone who has lost patience for a moment, but with the sustained ferocity of someone who had been waiting for an excuse. And then her hands went to his throat.

Jacob could not cry out properly. He could only struggle, small and terrified, his feet scrabbling against the grass.

In the neighbouring garden, a boy named Yusuf was watching.

Yusuf, witnessing the distressing scene unfolding before him, instinctively rushed to his mother for help, unable to ignore what was happening to a child his own age.

His mother, Mrs. Humaira, came fast — through the gate, across the garden, without hesitation, driven by the particular velocity of a woman who has seen something that cannot be unseen and has decided in the same instant what she is going to do about it. She pulled the nanny away. She gathered Jacob into her arms.

He clung to her.

He pressed his face against her shoulder and held on with everything he had, shaking too hard to speak, and Mrs. Humaira held him back and spoke to him softly — *you're safe, you're safe, I have you.*

She called the police without letting go of him.

When the officers arrived and the nanny was taken away — the maid alongside her, complicit in her silence — they attempted to take Jacob into protective custody. Thomas was abroad. There was no one else. Jacob understood none of the procedural necessity of what was happening. He only understood that the woman holding him was safe, and that they were trying to take him away from her.

He fought them with everything a four-year-old has.

It took time, and it took care, and when they finally carried him away, Mrs. Humaira stood in the garden and watched, and the expression on her face was the kind that stays with a person.

The call reached Thomas like a physical blow.

He moved immediately — cancelled everything, booked the first available flight, sat through twelve hours of travel with the specific torment of a parent who cannot get to their child fast enough. When he finally walked into the police station and saw Jacob, he stopped.

The boy sitting there was not the Jacob he had left behind.

He was four years old and he looked like someone who had been frightened for a very long time. He barely spoke. When he did, the words came out carefully, slowly, as though speech itself had become something to be cautious about.

Thomas crossed the room and pulled him close and held him for a long time without saying anything.

On the drive home, Thomas tried to talk. He asked simple questions and made gentle comments. He spoke softly, hoping to make things feel normal again. Jacob sat quietly next to him. Thomas kept talking, because he did not want it to be quiet.

At home, getting Jacob to eat was a negotiation conducted entirely in patience — small mouthfuls, slow encouragement, Thomas sitting across from his son and willing him gently toward each bite. Afterwards, he did not leave Jacob to sleep alone. He lay down beside him in the dark, and Jacob curled against him and trembled even in sleep, and Thomas stayed awake and watched over him and let the guilt do what it was going to do.

The room around them was extraordinary. Superhero murals on the walls, painted in bright colour. Furniture chosen for comfort and beauty. Toys in every corner — cars and figures and puzzles and soft things, an abundance of objects selected by a father who wanted his son to have everything. It was the kind of room you design when you love a child and believe that love can be expressed through provision, through the careful arrangement of a beautiful environment, through ensuring that everything *material* is in place.

Thomas looked at it in the dim light and understood, with a clarity that hurt in proportion to how long it had taken to arrive, that he had confused two things that are not the same.

He had given Jacob a prince's room. He had not given Jacob safety. He had given Jacob toys and a comfortable home. He had not given Jacob someone who was simply, reliably *there* — not as an arrangement, not on a schedule, not as a hired responsibility, but as a permanent and unconditional presence. He had brought his son into the world through careful planning, through contracts and agencies and the efficient management of a complex process, and he had believed, somewhere underneath everything, that careful planning was the same as love.

It was not.

A mother's warmth cannot be sourced. A child's need to feel held is not a logistical problem with a logistical solution. Thomas had tried to solve for everything except the thing that mattered most, and his son, four years old, trembling in his sleep in a beautiful room full of toys, was the consequence.

He lay in the dark and listened to Jacob breathe and made himself sit with the full weight of what he had done. Not to punish himself — guilt without action is just a feeling — but because he owed Jacob the honesty of looking at it clearly.

Whatever came next, he would not look away again.

The following morning, he took Jacob to visit the neighbours.

Mrs. Humaira opened the door, and before Thomas could properly begin his thanks, Yusuf appeared behind her and looked at Jacob with the frank, uncomplicated interest that small children bring to potential friends. Within minutes, both boys were on the carpet together, surrounded by toys, and Yusuf was pulling open a cupboard and presenting Jacob with one thing after another — *this one, look at this one* — with the generous enthusiasm of a child who has not yet learned to be possessive about what he has. Jacob received each offering carefully, and then, slowly, began to smile.

Thomas watched his son and felt something loosen in his chest.

When he learned, during the conversation, that it was Yusuf — four years old, just a child in a neighbouring garden — who had run to get his mother, who had set everything in motion that had saved Jacob, Thomas found he could not immediately speak. He looked at the small boy on the carpet, currently demonstrating the correct way to make a toy car jump off a cushion, and felt a gratitude that had no adequate expression.

He talked to Yusuf's parents more openly than he had talked to anyone in a long time. Something about their home made honesty feel safe. Yusuf's father was a university professor, measured and kind. Mrs. Humaira had been a teacher and had chosen, deliberately, to pull back from full-time work because she had decided that her children's upbringing was where she most needed to be. This was not a sacrifice she seemed to resent. It was simply the priority she had set, and the home it had produced was visible evidence of that choice.

When Thomas told them about Jacob — all of it, the surrogacy, Amelia, the shape of the life his son had been living — Mrs. Humaira listened without judgment. But when she understood that Jacob would never know anything about his mother, that there was no mother to know, her face did something quiet and sad. She felt, Thomas could see, the full weight of it — not as a criticism of him exactly, but as a grief for the child. For what Jacob had been asked to grow up without.

In the days that followed, a friendship formed between the two families with the natural ease of things that were always going to happen. Thomas asked, hesitantly, whether they might occasionally check on Jacob when he was travelling. Mrs. Humaira said yes before he had finished the sentence.

Then she said something that stopped him: *"If you're comfortable, Jacob can stay with us sometimes. He's always welcome here."*

Thomas felt lighter after as he returned home than he had in years.

Jacob, for his part, had already made his own decision about Yusuf's house.

The two boys started playschool together, walked home together, and every afternoon Jacob went directly next door. Mrs. Humaira fed them both lunch — the same food, the same table, the same easy warmth — and Jacob ate with the appetite of a child who is comfortable, which was something Thomas had not seen often enough. Thomas tried, gently, to explain that it wasn't quite polite to have lunch at someone's home every single day. Jacob listened attentively and then went back the next afternoon anyway.

He was four. He knew what he needed.

At Yusuf's house there was a mother who noticed you. There was a friend who shared his toys without being asked. There was an elder sister who included him in whatever she was doing. There was a father who laughed and played and got down on the floor. The house had the particular atmosphere of a place where people genuinely like being together — not because everything is perfect, but because there is love in the structure of it, in the routines and the meals and the small daily attentions that add up, over time, to a child who feels safe.

Jacob's own house had a professional caretaker who came and went on schedule.

He was four years old and he understood the difference completely, even without the words to say so.

He still had faint, unclear memories of Amelia. The image of a woman, glamorous and a little distant, who had called him her son in photographs. Every so often, out of nowhere, he would turn to Thomas and ask the question with the simple directness of a child who has not yet learned to protect people from their own questions.

"Where is my mother?"

And Thomas, every time, would find some gentle way around it. A deflection, a distraction, a promise of something else. He never lied. He never told the truth either. He was a man standing at the edge of a conversation he did not know how to begin, with a child who deserved better than silence and was patient enough, for now, to wait.

On an ordinary afternoon, in a grocery store, between the fruit aisle and the checkout, Thomas was moving through the shelves with half his attention on the list in his hand when he heard Jacob's voice — high and urgent and full of something that made him drop the basket immediately.

"Mommy! Mommy!"

He pushed through the aisle and saw Jacob running, his small legs carrying him as fast as they could toward a woman near the entrance. Before Thomas could reach him, Jacob had caught her by the coat, both hands gripping the fabric, his face turned upward with an expression of such raw, unguarded hope that it was almost unbearable to witness.

The woman turned around.

It was Amelia.

Thomas stopped. The world did one of those strange slow things it sometimes does in moments of shock, where everything continues moving at normal speed but your understanding of it lags behind by several seconds. Amelia. Here. Jacob had recognised her somehow — some fragment of memory, a shape or a scent or the particular way she moved — and had run to her with everything he had.

Amelia looked down at the small boy holding her coat and pulled it free from his hands.

"What kind of misbehaviour is this?"

Her voice was sharp and cold in the way of someone who has been inconvenienced by a stranger. She was with a man — a boyfriend, clearly — and her expression contained no flicker of recognition, no softening, nothing that acknowledged that this child had once been photographed in her arms for an audience of thousands.

Thomas reached Jacob's side. He had nothing to say. What was there to say?

Amelia looked at both of them with an irritation that had no room in it for guilt, but she could not say anything on this cute and desperate mistake of Jacob. She turned to her boyfriend and walked away.

Jacob stood very still.

He did not cry. He did not say anything to Thomas about what he was feeling, and Thomas did not push him — partly because he didn't know how, and partly because some moments are too delicate for the wrong words. They finished the shopping in near silence and drove home, and the question Jacob had been asking for years — *where is my mother* — received, that afternoon, its answer. Not in words. In a coat pulled away from small hands, and a woman's back retreating through a door.

He never asked the question again.

Time, as it does, kept moving. And in its movement, it brought Jacob things that mattered.

Yusuf, most of all.

They had grown from two four-year-olds on a carpet with toy cars into teenagers who understood each other the way people do when they have shared enough of the formative years to know each other's defaults. They were fifteen now, both of them bright and curious, both pulled toward science with enthusiasm. Mrs. Humaira had done that — guided them with the patient rigour of someone who loves both her subject and her students.

For Jacob, Mrs. Humaira had become something he didn't have a precise word for. *Mom* was the word he used, frankly and naturally, and she received it without fuss. She had taught him to organise his days, to eat properly, to sit with a difficult problem until it yielded rather than abandoning it. She had filled in the gaps with the steady, undemonstrative care of a woman who simply decided, years ago, that this boy needed someone and that she was available to be that person.

Their two families had woven themselves together in the way of people who genuinely enjoy each other's company. Christmas at Jacob's house — the decorations planned jointly, the menu negotiated, Thomas watching from the doorway with the contentment of a man who has been given back something he thought he'd lost. Eid at Mrs. Humaira's — the food, the warmth, the festive atmosphere that Jacob stepped into and was simply, visibly, happy.

The boys had a running joke about their names — Jacob and Yusuf, the same soul in two languages, the father and the son across two scriptures. They delivered the punchline with the timing of people who have told it many times and still find it funny, which is the truest sign of a good friendship.

Beneath the teasing was something real: two young men who had learned each other's faiths with genuine curiosity and genuine respect, who had discovered that understanding someone's beliefs is one of the most direct routes to understanding the person themselves.

One evening they were studying together in Jacob's living room — a science project, exam season pressing close, the lamp on and the room quiet with the specific concentration of fifteen-year-olds who are taking something seriously.

Jacob stretched back in his chair, looked toward the cabinet in the corner, and got the particular expression that Yusuf had learned to be cautious about — the one that meant an idea had arrived and was being considered more seriously than it deserved.

"Hey," Jacob said. *"Dad's not home. What do you think about trying some whisky?"*

Yusuf looked up from his notebook. *"Are you being serious right now?"*

"Just a sip. Everyone in our class has already — "

"Jacob."

"— it's not a big deal, it's just to see what it's like, and honestly even among Muslims these days it's pretty — "

"Jacob, stop." Yusuf put his pen down. *"No. I don't want to. And I'd rather you didn't either."*

But Jacob was already at the cabinet. He had the bottle out, the casualness of his movements slightly too deliberate, in the way of someone performing confidence they don't entirely feel. He poured two small glasses and held one out. Yusuf looked at it. He looked at Jacob's face. He thought about the line between not wanting to seem childish and not wanting to do something he knew was wrong, and he found, in that moment, that the line was thinner than he had realised.

"Just to see," he said quietly, and took the glass.

They clinked, in a parody of something adult, and drank.

The whisky hit Yusuf's throat like a correction. Bitter, sharp, burning — his face did everything his manners were trying to prevent it from doing, and he put the glass down immediately.

"That's awful," he said, with the honest disgust of someone who has just discovered that a supposedly sophisticated thing is simply unpleasant. *"How does anyone drink that willingly?"*

Jacob laughed, but without the triumph he had been going for. He had expected something revelatory — some understanding of why adults chose this, why his classmates bragged about it. What he found was a bad taste and a faint unease that was already spreading somewhere underneath the laughter.

The room went quieter than it had been before.

Yusuf wiped his mouth and said, without drama: *"I don't think we should do that again."*

Jacob nodded, slowly, still looking at the glass. He didn't have a clever response. The cabinet that had seemed like a symbol of freedom fifteen minutes ago was just a cabinet again, with a bottle in it that tasted like a bad idea.

For Yusuf, the discomfort settled into something useful — a reminder that the voice of conscience is easy to negotiate with in the abstract and considerably harder to ignore once you've already acted against it. For Jacob, it was quieter than that. Just a small, unwelcome knowledge that in trying to seem older than he was, he had done something he was not proud of.

Neither of them mentioned it again. But neither of them forgot it either.

For Jacob, the guilt was uncomfortable and then, gradually, manageable. He was fifteen, the world was large, there were other things to think about. He moved on in the way that teenagers move on from things they don't want to examine too closely.

For Yusuf, it was different.

The weight of what he had done did not lift. If anything, it settled deeper with each passing day — not because the act itself was enormous in the world's eyes, but because of what it meant inside his. He had done something that Allah had clearly and unambiguously forbidden. He knew this. He had always known this. And he had done it anyway, talked himself into it with the threadbare logic of *just once, just to see, everyone else has* — the exact reasoning that sounds reasonable in the moment and hollow immediately afterwards. For Yusuf, the Qur'an provided foundational guidance, shaping his identity and worldview. To act against it was not just to break a rule. It was to break faith with something he genuinely loved.

He began to pray more, which helped a little. He asked Allah for forgiveness, which helped more. But the guilt clung, and beneath it was a second fear, sharper in its own way: *what will my parents think of me when they find out?*

That fear was the one that really did the damage. It crept into his concentration during class, dismantled his focus, pulled him away from his friends — even from Jacob, which was its own kind of loss. The bright, cheerful, endlessly curious Yusuf that his teachers had always relied upon began to dim. His grades slipped quietly. His smiles arrived less readily. Mrs. Humaira noticed and attributed it to adolescence, that catch-all explanation for things adults don't quite want to investigate. But at home, where his parents knew him better than anyone, the change was impossible to dismiss.

One evening, his father sat down beside him.

Not with a question prepared, not with an accusation waiting in the wings. Just — sat down, close, and was present.

"Assalamualaikum, Abba," Yusuf said quietly.

"Wa Alaikum Assalam, beta."

The clock ticked. Outside, the street carried on with its ordinary evening business. Then his father said, gently and without pressure: *"If something is troubling you, you can trust me. I promise I'll do everything I can to help. And if you wish, I won't even tell your Ammi. But my son — unless you share what's weighing on you, how can we find a way through it together?"*

Something in Yusuf broke open.

He had been carrying it alone for months, turning it over and over in a closed space, and here was his father, offering him a way out that required nothing except honesty. He cried before he could speak — the particular relief of someone who has been holding on too tightly for too long — and then, through the tears, he told his father everything.

His father listened without interrupting. His face, when Yusuf finally looked at it, held no anger. Only compassion, and something that looked very much like love that has not been diminished by disappointment.

"My dear child," his father said, drawing him close, *"the remorse in your heart is not a sign of weakness. It is a sign of how deeply you love Allah. Everyone stumbles. What matters is whether you turn back. Have you been asking Him for forgiveness?"*

Yusuf nodded, still unable to speak properly.

"Then He has already heard you." His father held him while he cried. *"I'm proud of you, Yusuf. Not for the mistake — but for the honesty. That takes courage."*

The months that followed were a quiet restoration. Yusuf prayed with more intention. He returned to his studies with renewed determination, as though the act of being forgiven — by Allah, by his father, and slowly by himself — had freed up something in him that had been locked. When the results came at the end of those years, they reflected a young man who had found his footing again. He earned his place at a prestigious university, and he left for it carrying lessons about guilt and repentance and the specific grace of being known by someone who loves you anyway.

The two friends moved to different cities for their studies. When they returned home during holidays they met, briefly, warmly, affectionately. Neither said aloud how much he missed the other. Neither needed to.

It was during one long Christmas holiday, both of them home at the same time, that they found themselves in Thomas's garden in the late afternoon, the old ease returning as it always did within minutes of being together again. They talked about university, about mutual friends, about the particular strangeness of becoming adults in a world that keeps presenting new versions of choices you thought you'd already made.

Then Jacob went quiet in a way that Yusuf recognised — not the comfortable silence of two friends at rest, but the effortful quiet of someone working up to something.

He told Yusuf about the substances. About how it had started casually enough, the way these things always start — a social thing, a university thing, something everyone seemed to be doing. About how it had stopped being casual without him quite noticing. About how his concentration had deteriorated, his grades had slipped, and a depression had settled over him that he couldn't seem to lift himself out of regardless of how hard he tried. He had friends at university — plenty of them — but none who knew him the way Yusuf knew him. None with whom honesty felt safe in the same way.

When he finished talking, his face was wet.

"Please help me, Yusuf. I don't know how to get out of this. I feel lost. I want to stop — I genuinely want to stop — but I can't do it alone."

Yusuf sat with everything his friend had just handed him. He felt the weight of it — the worry for Jacob, the urgency of it. He had been in a smaller version of this place once. He knew what it felt like to be trapped by something you were ashamed of, to carry guilt that had no outlet, to need someone to know before the knowing could kill you.

He put his hand on Jacob's shoulder.

"We'll face this together," he said. *"I promise."*

Before either of them could say more, Thomas's voice came from the house — warm and unhurried, carrying across the garden the way familiar voices do. *"Jacob! Yusuf! Come inside, my children — dinner is ready!"*

Jacob wiped his face quickly and looked at Yusuf with the fear of a son who has been the source of his father's pride and cannot bear the thought of becoming the source of his grief. *"Please don't tell Papa. Not yet. He's always believed in me. I can't — I don't know what it would do to him."*

"I won't," Yusuf said simply. *"Not yet. But Jacob — we will find a way through this."*

Thomas called again, warmer this time, with the mock impatience of a man who is genuinely happy: *"It's getting cold, you two!"*

They went inside.

The house was bright and fragrant and full — Thomas, Mrs. Humaira, Yusuf's father, the Christmas lights casting everything in their particular warmth. They ate together, all of them, and laughed at things that weren't that funny but felt funny because of who was in the room, and the evening had the quality of something that would be remembered. Jacob, who had been carrying so much for so long, felt it lift slightly in the presence of these people — his father, his almost-mother, his best friend — and allowed himself, just for the length of a Christmas dinner, to feel held.

Tomorrow the problem would still be there. But tonight, he was not alone.

The Christmas lights were still up when Yusuf sat alone in his room and tried to work out what to do.

Jacob had asked him for one thing — silence — and Yusuf had promised it. But silence, he was beginning to understand, was not the same as loyalty. Sometimes it was the opposite. He turned the problem over carefully, the way his father had taught him to turn problems over, looking at each face of it honestly, and what he kept arriving at was this: without professional help, Jacob was not going to get better. And without Thomas knowing, professional help was not possible. Jacob had drawn a line and asked Yusuf to respect it, but the line was drawn in the wrong place, and a real friend does not simply stand on the respectful side of a line while his friend drowns.

He was still sitting with this when Jacob walked in.

One look was enough. Jacob's face was pale, his hands unsteady, his eyes carrying that particular restless desperation that Yusuf had seen worsen over the past days. Before Yusuf could speak, Jacob was already asking — pleading, his voice stripped of its usual composure — for Yusuf to get him something. Anything. Just to get through the day.

Yusuf stood up.

"Sit down, Jacob." His voice was calm but it left no room for negotiation. *"Sit down and listen to me. This ends now."*

Jacob sat, appearing as a restless, needy child. Yusuf, feeling the depth of his friend's suffering, made his decision.

"I know you," Yusuf said. *"Better than anyone. And I am not going to stand here and watch you disappear. You are one of the most brilliant people I have ever known, and that is not a small thing — that is your life, Jacob, and it is worth fighting for."*

He told Jacob his plan. Transfer to Yusuf's university, where a rehabilitation programme was available. The academic record Jacob had built before the addiction — the certificates, the awards, the evidence of who he actually was — would be enough to secure a place. Yusuf would handle the arrangements. Jacob would not have to face any of it alone.

Jacob was quiet for a long time.

Then he said, softly, that it wouldn't work. That he didn't believe he could do it. He still had the fear what will happen if his father – Thomas got to know about his addiction. Yusuf said

"My family won't know the real reason, I promise you that. But Jacob — your father has to know. Not to shame you. Because he loves you, and without him we cannot do this properly. And think about it honestly: if you cannot tell your own father, who in this world will care enough to actually help you?"

He let that sit.

"He will not be disappointed in you for struggling," Yusuf said. *"He will be proud of you for deciding to fight."*

It took time. It took the rest of that afternoon and most of the next day, the conversation returning and retreating like a tide, Jacob's resistance softening in increments. But Yusuf was patient in the way of someone who has already decided the outcome and is simply waiting for his friend to arrive at the same place.

When Thomas heard everything, he did not fall apart.

He sat with it. He looked at his son, perhaps for the first time in too long — and then he looked at Yusuf, this young man who had been part of their lives since he was four years old and had just demonstrated more wisdom and more love than most adults manage in a lifetime.

"I am truly glad," Thomas said quietly, *"that my son has a friend like you."*

He arranged the rehabilitation centre himself, in Yusuf's city, without delay and without hesitation, because whatever his failures as a father had been — and he knew them, he had counted them — abandoning his son in the moment Jacob finally asked for help was not going to be added to the list.

Six months later. It was not easy. Rehabilitation never is — it is unglamorous and gruelling and requires a person to sit with the full honest inventory of themselves without flinching away from any of it. Jacob did this work. Some days were better than others. Some days he could see the person he was trying to become clearly, and other days that person felt impossibly far away.

But Yusuf came regularly. He sat with Jacob and they talked about science, about university, about the future — not because the past didn't matter but because Yusuf understood that the mind needs somewhere to go, and he kept pointing Jacob's mind forward. They sketched out plans. They worked through problems together. Yusuf treated Jacob not as a patient to be managed but as the brilliant, capable person he had always known him to be, and that — more than any programme or protocol — was perhaps what healed him most.

Jacob lost an academic year. He gained considerably more than that in return.

When he finally walked onto Yusuf's university campus, he looked around at it with the clear eyes of someone who knows exactly what it cost to get there and is not taking a moment of it lightly. He had fought for this. Not alone — never alone — but the fight had been his, and the victory was his, and he wore it quietly and well.

Eight years on.

Both of them are settled now — careers, lives, the ordinary beautiful complexity of adulthood. The world is busy and demanding and pulls people in directions that childhood friendships often cannot survive. Most don't. The drift happens gradually, then completely, and one day you realise that someone who once knew everything about you has become a person you occasionally see in photographs.

Jacob and Yusuf did not drift.

They remained, across the distance and the years and the separate trajectories of their lives, genuinely present to each other — not just in sentiment but in the actual ongoing fact of a friendship that neither of them treated as something that could be allowed to fade. There was always a place for it, always time made for it, always the understanding between them that what they had was not easily replaced and should not be taken for granted.

And when Christmas came — every year, without fail — it was as though a window opened somewhere and the air that came through it smelled of Jacob's house and Yusuf's garden and all the years that had made them who they were.

Their friendship had begun with a four-year-old boy watching through a garden fence and running to get his mother.

It had survived a grocery store, a whisky bottle, a rehab centre, and eight years of separate lives.

It was, by any measure, the real thing which will remain with them to cherish for the rest of their lives.

* * * * *

Chapter 5

Ayesha – A Life Worth Living

Ayesha was six years old and she was, by general agreement, impossible not to love.

It wasn't anything she did deliberately — she was simply the kind of child who makes a room feel warmer by being in it. Round-faced and bright-eyed, with the unselfconscious sweetness of a child who has grown up feeling entirely secure, she moved through the world as though she owns it, which, as far as her father was concerned, was more or less the correct understanding of the situation.

Mr. Mustafa adored his daughter in the uncomplicated way of fathers who have not bothered to pretend otherwise. Ayesha knew this, accepted it as the natural order of things.

Her brother Hussain was eleven — old enough to roll his eyes occasionally, young enough to still be caught enjoying the same things as his little sister when he thought no one was looking. Their home in Delhi was the kind of household that hums with quiet contentment: good food, purposeful routines, parents who talked to each other and meant it. Mr. Mustafa worked long hours at a large private firm and carried the responsibility of it steadily, without complaint. Mrs. Asia ran the home with the focused attention of someone who has made a deliberate choice about where her energy belongs and has no regrets about it.

She was educated — more than capable of a career — and had chosen, with clear eyes and genuine conviction, to be present for her children instead. The results were visible in Hussain and Ayesha: children who were bright and curious and well-mannered, who excelled at school not because they were pushed but because they had been given a home in which learning felt natural. Mrs. Asia regarded this as the most meaningful work she had ever done, and she was right.

Both children attended one of Delhi's finest schools. Both had inherited something of their mother's focus and their father's warmth. Life, for this family, was not without its ordinary worries — but it was good, and they knew it, and they were grateful.

One evening, Mr. Mustafa and Mrs. Asia sat together after the children had gone to bed, talking about the future in the way that parents do — higher education, savings, the possibility of sending Hussain and Ayesha abroad one day. They were planners by nature, both of them, not because they believed the future was entirely in their hands, but because they understood that trusting in Allah and making thoughtful decisions were not opposites. You did your best with the wisdom you had, and you held the rest lightly.

There was, however, one matter on which Mrs. Asia had begun to feel a quiet, persistent frustration.

The house.

Mr. Mustafa was meticulous about almost everything — the children's school, their activities, their health, the smallest details of their upbringing. But whenever Mrs. Asia raised the subject of buying a home of their own, he would redirect the conversation. A gentle subject change here, a *we'll discuss it properly soon* there. The children were growing. Time was moving. And still — nothing.

What she didn't know was that there was a surprise ready to be revealed.

Mr. Mustafa had already bought the house. He had booked it quietly, some time ago, with the particular pleasure of a man who is keeping a secret he very much looks forward to revealing. It was in Nainital — the place where he had grown up, where the hills came down to the lake and the air had a quality that Delhi air simply could not match. His dream, nurtured since childhood, was to return there after retirement. To live quietly, close to nature, in a place that had always felt like the truest version of home.

Nainital was also, for different and more immediate reasons, the children's favourite place in the world.

Every year, when the Delhi heat became genuinely unreasonable and school broke for the holidays, the family moved — first to Ajmer, where Mrs. Asia's mother and brother lived and where Ayesha and Hussain were received with the particular enthusiasm of grandparents and relatives who have been waiting months for exactly this visit. Then northward to Nainital, to Mr. Mustafa's mother, to the cool air and the familiar smell of the hills and the grandmother's kitchen.

This summer followed the same beloved pattern.

The house in Nainital was modest — three rooms, a grandmother who filled every corner of it, an uncle's family who occupied the rest. The room that technically belonged to Mr. Mustafa had long been made available to his younger brother's children during the long stretches when he wasn't there. He had offered this without a second thought, and the offer had been accepted without ceremony, which was the way things worked in a family that functioned well.

When the family arrived, the house came alive. There were greetings and embraces and the immediate smell of something good being cooked, and Ayesha mingled up with her cousins and ensued the cute little ruckus.

Mrs. Asia had brought gifts — chosen carefully, as she always did, with the particular thoughtfulness of someone who takes the act of giving seriously. For the grandmother, an expensive shawl and warm woolens suited to Nainital's cool evenings. For the aunt, a silk sari in soft pastels. For the uncle, a fine perfume and shirts he would actually wear. For the children, branded clothes and toys and chocolates, distributed with the joy of an aunt who has been looking forward to this moment.

The room filled with the pleasure of unwrapping. The grandmother held her shawl with genuine delight. The uncle examined his perfume with appreciation. The children tore into their chocolates immediately, which was the correct response.

Ayesha's aunt accepted the gift with smile on her face but behind that smile there was calculation going on. The gifts were lovely, but Mr. Mustafa was, by the aunt's estimation, a wealthy man. Surely a wealthy man's wife could have done a little more.

The aunt, for her part, had a rather different approach to gifts. What Ayesha and Hussain received from her in return tended toward the ordinary — items chosen more for ease than care, things the children already had in considerably better versions back home in Delhi.

Mrs. Asia and Mr. Mustafa had different philosophy towards gifting. They bought for others what they would buy for themselves. This was, according to them, the honest way of gifting. It did not account for other people's expectations, but it gave them the satisfaction that they had done the right thing.

Both Ayesha and Hussain were trained by their parents to accept gifts with a big smile and show gratitude towards elder who are gifting them.

Mr. Mustafa had a secret, and keeping it was becoming increasingly enjoyable.

He told everyone he was travelling to Nainital for work — an official project, that's why the trip this time was unusually long. Mrs. Asia accepted this without suspicion because her husband was, by nature, a man whose work occasionally required his presence elsewhere. Ayesha and Hussain were simply pleased that the Nainital visit was happening at all. Nobody asked too many questions, which suited Mr. Mustafa perfectly. The house he had quietly purchased needed renovations, paperwork, signatures — that also required him to be away from the family for several hours in the day.

The first ten days passed pleasantly enough. The house was full in the way it always was when the family visited — warm, slightly chaotic, anchored by the grandmother's presence and the general goodwill of people who are genuinely glad to see each other.

Then, gradually, the atmosphere began to shift.

The room where Mr. Mustafa was staying was, technically, his, but was occupied by his brother's children during the long months of his absence. As the days were passing by, it was becoming increasingly difficult for Zulekha, Ayesha's aunt to bear the burden of guests. Although she did not say anything, the tension in the house slowly began to rise.

One day, Mr. Mustafa mentioned, in the easy conversational way of someone raising a practical matter, that the water pressure throughout the house had dropped significantly. The plumbing, he said, probably needed attention. It was a straightforward observation about a shared problem.

Zulekha looked up and said, with a hint of frustration in her voice: *"Yes, of course, brother — please go ahead and get it fixed. It's your house too, after all."*

The words were technically agreeable. The tone was not.

Mr. Mustafa did not like the comment at all, instead of reacting, he took a deep breadth and with full calmness said:

"Zulekha, I have always contributed more to the upkeep of this house than anyone else, even though I don't live here. Six months ago, when the house was painted, I paid sixty-five thousand of the one lakh rupees it cost. I am the eldest son of this house and I understand my responsibilities. Please don't tell me what I should or shouldn't do regarding my own home."

It was said without heat, which made it land harder than shouting would have.

Zulekha left the room. The evening went quiet in the particular way of a house in which something has been said that cannot be unsaid, tension was in the air but conversations were going on though at a shallow level. Six or seven days still remained before the family was due to return to Delhi. They felt, suddenly, like a longer stretch.

It was Ayesha's uncle — Mr. Mustafa's younger brother — who took the initiatives to bring the peace back. He made efforts every day to lighten the environment: sometimes he took all the children out for ice cream, other times he brought fresh fruits and chocolates home to cheer everyone up. Slowly, his kind gestures began to have an effect. Seeing his younger brother's dedication and efforts to keep the family united, Mr. Mustafa felt deeply moved and proud. Within two days, the atmosphere in the house returned to normal. Smiles replaced the awkward silence, and everyone began talking to each other warmly again.

Meanwhile, Mr. Mustafa also managed to finish all his house documentation and renovation-related work successfully. With the paperwork completed and the family tensions resolved, he finally felt a sense of peace and satisfaction.

The day Mr. Mustafa was all set to return to Delhi, his brother came to him and made a request.

Ten lakh rupees, he said. For the business. An expansion he had been thinking about.

Mr. Mustafa considered this carefully. *"I don't have that kind of cash available right now,"* he said. *"But I can arrange a loan through a friend — the money would be there, it would just come through him."*

His brother's expression changed.

"You have a good job — and the amount I am asking is not a big deal for you brother?"

Mr. Mustafa looked at him steadily. *"You will get the money. What does it matter whether it comes directly from me or through a friend? When you are in position to return, return it."*

He said it gently. But he had noticed something in his brother's manner — perhaps an assumption that the money, once given, would not need to be returned. His brother had not liked it, which told Mr. Mustafa something he filed away without comment.

The family returned to Delhi. The journey home was quieter than usual, and Mr. Mustafa sat with his thoughts

— the strange slight bitterness of watching family behave in ways you did not expect from them and the private gratitude for his own small household, his wife and children, the uncomplicated love of it.

Back in Delhi, he settled into his routines. The new house had drawn heavily on their finances that year — more than he had anticipated — and the education savings plan he had intended to start for Ayesha and Hussain was quietly postponed. *Next year*, he told himself. There was time.

When his brother asked for the money, Mr. Mustafa sent five lakh rupees — half of what had been requested, and, though he did not say this aloud, the exact sum he had set aside for his children's education fund. He had prayed about it and decided. To give for the sake of Allah's pleasure, even when the timing was difficult, was not irresponsibility. It was faith. He trusted that other arrangements could be made for the children when the time came.

His brother received the money and thought, privately, that patience and persistence with a generous elder brother was a reliable strategy. He did not know that what he held was his niece and nephew's education fund. He did not think to ask.

Winter came to Delhi slowly and then all at once, the fog settling over the city in the way it does — thick and unhurried, softening everything at the edges. Mr. Mustafa had been planning a surprise for months. A winter trip to Nainital, the whole family together, and at the end of it — the house. The freshly renovated rooms, the hill air, the view he had been imagining sharing with Mrs. Asia and the children since the day he signed the papers.

He had pictured Ayesha's face when she understood. He had pictured Mrs. Asia's expression — the particular satisfaction of a woman who has been patient a long time and is finally shown why.

But fate, which does not consult our pictures of things, had already written a different chapter.

On the evening of December 20th, Mr. Mustafa did not come home.

His car was involved in an accident on the way back from work. He died at the scene.

The news arrived and broke everything at once.

For Mrs. Asia, it was not like receiving information. It was like the ground simply stopping. One moment the world had a shape she recognised — husband, children, home, plans, a future that made sense — and the next it did not. Ayesha and Hussain, who did not yet have the vocabulary for what had happened, understood it in their bodies before they understood it in their minds: something essential was gone, and the space it left was enormous.

Mr. Mustafa was taken to Nainital, to the hills he had loved his whole life, and buried there. The mountain air was cold and still. The silence around the grave was the kind that presses on you.

A week passed. Then the relatives began to ask, with the practical urgency of people who are uncomfortable with open-ended situations, what Mrs. Asia intended to do. Would she stay in Delhi? Move to Nainital? Something needed to be decided.

Mrs. Asia had no answer yet. She was still inside the first grief, the raw and formless kind, where decisions feel like mountains and every word costs more than you have.

Zulekha, however, had already decided.

She did not say it plainly — she was too careful for that — but her discomfort was visible in the way she held herself, in the direction of her glances toward the room where Mrs. Asia and the children were staying.

She inserted herself into the conversation with the timing of someone who has been waiting for an opening.

"Why would the children stay here?" she said, her voice carrying the particular brightness of someone presenting selfishness as common sense. *"They go to excellent schools in Delhi. Why would Bhabhi bring them all the way to Nainital? And besides — this house is far too small."*

Everyone in the room understood what had just been said. No one said so aloud. The polite silence was its own kind of commentary.

December moved slowly, the way months do when you are grieving and the ordinary passage of time feels like an affront. The days blurred. The household in Delhi continued generating its expenses — rent, electricity, school fees — with the indifferent reliability of systems that do not adjust for tragedy. Mrs. Asia looked at the bills and understood, practically and without self-pity, that she would need to work. But first she needed to know where home was going to be. Not just a roof — a place with people around her, support, the safety of family.

She thought of Ajmer. Her mother, her brother — surely they would say *come, come immediately, we'll figure it out together.*

She called her mother and told her she was thinking of moving there with the children after the school exams in March.

Her mother was quiet for a moment. Then she said, carefully: *"My child — it's one thing for you to visit during holidays. That is always welcome. But if you come to live here permanently, things between you and your brother and his wife will become difficult eventually. Nobody is truly comfortable with that kind of arrangement. I am their grandmother — I can put up with a great deal — but a child's real home is with the paternal family. That is where you should go."*

Mrs. Asia sat with the phone in her hand and said nothing for a moment.

She had been expecting her mother to say *come at once, I'll send your brother for you.* The gap between what she had expected and what she had received was wide enough to fall into. She thought, with a bitterness she could not entirely suppress, that perhaps her mother's answer might have been different if Ayesha's maternal grandfather had still been alive — if there had been a man in that house to take a stand.

She called her brother and told him what their mother had said. He listened, and then said, with the measured tone of a man managing his own inconvenience: *"Mother isn't entirely wrong. But if you really want to come, tell me and I'll make arrangements."* A pause. *"I'm tied up right now. I'll call you later."*

He did not call.

A week passed. The silence from her brother settled over her like cold weather. She understood then that her family was not going to step forward. They were not cruel people. They simply had their own lives, their own arrangements, their own calculations, and a widowed sister with two children did not fit comfortably into any of them.

She called Ayesha's grandmother in Nainital and told her plainly: after the exams, she intended to move there and enrol the children in school.

The answer came back sharp and swift. *"Why would you come here? What is there for you in Nainital? Stay in Delhi. Keep your job there. The children have grown up in Delhi — your coming will only cause unnecessary trouble."*

Mrs. Asia heard the message underneath the words. She did not call again.

She sat that afternoon and thought about the man she had lost.

Mr. Mustafa had spent his life stepping forward for people. But now that his own family is in trouble and needed help, not one hand reached out to help. The remark only layered more sorrow on Mrs. Asia's heart.

The grief and the abandonment arrived together, and Mrs. Asia allowed herself, finally, to weep.

Ayesha and Hussain, seeing their mother's tears, began to cry too.

She held them both close for a long time. Then she lifted her head.

She thought of her husband — of the way he had raised these children, of what he had wanted for them, of the quiet dignity with which he had moved through the world. She thought of what he would want her to do now, in this room, with these two small people looking at her face for instruction on how to be.

She wiped her own tears. Then, gently, she wiped theirs.

"We are each other's strength," she told them, her voice steady in the way of a woman who has decided something. *"We are strong. Beside Allah, we need no one else."*

She meant it. Not as comfort only, but as fact — as a declaration of the terms on which she intended to continue.

After the coldness she had received from both sides of the family, Mrs. Asia did not call again. She was a woman of dignity, and dignity, once a door has been clearly closed, does not knock twice.

She turned her attention to Delhi and to the practical work of rebuilding. She had started looking for a new school for Ayesha and Hussain, one with lower fees, and had already applied for teaching positions in two or three nearby schools. Mr. Mustafa had been a careful man; there were savings, not enormous, but real. The difficulty was that they had been put aside for the children's future, for university and what lay beyond it — not for now, not for rent and school fees and the monthly weight of ordinary life.

Mrs. Asia's new life had just begun — a life of struggle and silent determination. She spent her days visiting schools, collecting forms, preparing for interviews, and returning home exhausted but hopeful. Then, one afternoon near the end of March — the day of the children's result declaration — an unexpected visitor arrived. It was Mr. Hafeez, who had come all the way from Nainital.

Mr. Hafeez stood in the doorway. He had been Mr. Mustafa's closest friend — the kind of friendship that is less a choice than a fact of life, accumulated over so many years that the two men had simply become part of each other's furniture. He was carrying a thick file.

He sat down in the drawing room with the gravity of someone who has been waiting for the right moment to do something important.

"Bhabhi," he said gently, *"this house is yours."*

Mrs. Asia looked at him without understanding.

He opened the file. He explained, quietly and carefully, what her husband had been doing on all those trips to Nainital — the paperwork, the renovations, the decisions made about interiors and fittings. Mr. Mustafa had bought a house. He had been preparing it in secret for months, intending to bring his family there in December, to walk them through the door and watch their faces rearrange themselves into something he had been imagining for years.

"He wanted it to be a surprise," Mr. Hafeez said, and his voice shifted slightly on the last word. *"But in December, he left us instead."*

Mrs. Asia held the file against her chest and wept — not only from grief, but from the particular ache of understanding, fully and finally, what her husband had been building while she was busy being gently frustrated with him for avoiding the subject of houses. He had not been avoiding it. He had been constructing it, brick by brick, in secret, for love.

Mr. Hafeez called Ayesha and Hussain to him. He placed a hand on each of their shoulders with the tenderness of a man who understands exactly what these two have lost.

"Your father left you something beautiful," he told them. *"Your very own home. When you see it, you'll understand how much he loved you."*

He asked about their results — the exams had been declared that very day.

"Yes, Uncle," both children answered together. *"We passed."*

More than passed. Despite the grief they had lived through, their results were outstanding. Mrs. Asia looked at her children and felt, briefly and intensely, the pride of a parent who recognises that something they worked very hard to build has held.

Mr. Hafeez explained, gently, why he had waited until now to come. The iddat period — the time of mourning and withdrawal observed after a husband's death — had only recently concluded. He had not wanted to intrude on that sanctity, had waited with the file until the right moment arrived.

"Please think of me as your brother," he said. *"Mustafa and I were more than friends — you know that. Every decision about that house was made with you in mind. He chose everything according to your taste. He wanted you to walk in and feel, immediately, that it was home."*

He paused, and when he spoke again his voice was lower.

"Bhabhi — I know your in-laws well. I know his brother and his wife. They will never truly welcome you if you go to them. Mustafa knew this too. That is why he built this house — so that you and the children could live with dignity, without depending on anyone."

The words settled over Mrs. Asia like something warm. Her husband had known. He had seen clearly, and he had quietly arranged for her protection before the need for it had even arrived. His love had not ended with his life. It had simply taken a different form — a file in a friend's hands, a set of keys, a house in the hills waiting for them.

Mrs. Asia confided in Mr. Hafeez about her plans — she was thinking of transferring her children to a less expensive school and had also begun searching for a job herself.

He listened, then said warmly: *"Bhabhi, if you'll allow me — why not move to Nainital? Live in your own house. The children's academic record will open any school's door. And for work, you can search there as easily as here. My wife and I will be nearby. You need only ask."*

They were the words no relative had managed to say to her. Not her mother, not her brother, not her in-laws. A friend of her husband's — a man who owed her nothing — had said them without hesitation and without condition.

That night, after the children were asleep, Mrs. Asia sat alone and thanked Allah with the full weight of everything she had been carrying for months. The house felt like an answer to prayers she had not known how to articulate — prayers spoken in the dark of her grief, without shape or specific request, just the raw and wordless need of a woman trying to hold her family together. Allah had heard them before she had found the words. He had placed the answer in her husband's hands before the question had even arrived.

By the end of April, Delhi was packed up and left behind.

The house in Nainital was exactly as she had always dreamed for her children and her family — a cozy three-bedroom home with a lovely living area, a kitchen equipped with all the essentials, two balconies, a beautiful entrance, and of course, a breathtaking view of the mountains from every room.

Mr. Hafeez and his wife helped her immensely in settling down. Soon, Ayesha and Hussain were admitted into one of Nainital's most prestigious schools — even better than the one they had attended in Delhi.

Life for Mrs. Asia and her children began to feel like a dream. They could hardly believe how swiftly their troubles were fading away, one after another. But then, Allah's miracles often unfold just like that — quietly, beautifully, and completely.

Only one thing remained — Mrs. Asia's job. And after five or six months, that too was taken care of: she was offered a teaching position at a local school.

Ayesha and Hussain's maternal and paternal grandmothers often came to stay with them in their new home in Nainital. The peaceful atmosphere of the house, the laughter of the children, and the calm, organized rhythm of their lives brought both grandmothers great joy. They often sat together on the balcony, sipping tea, watching the sun sink behind the mountains, and thanking Allah for the serenity that had returned to the family after such dark and difficult times. On the other hand, Ayesha and Hussain's uncle and aunt could hardly believe how swiftly Mrs. Asia and her children had settled into their new lives — and that too, within just a year of Mr. Mustafa's passing.

Ayesha's aunt, Mrs. Zulaikha, had even begun taunting her husband. She would say sharply,

"Your brother was the wiser one — he left this world only after making sure his family was secure and well-provided for. And you? You're always troubled — sometimes because of your business losses, and sometimes because of complaints from your children's school!"

In truth, where arrogance and deceit take root, peace and blessings quietly slip away. Homes filled with pride and falsehood rarely see contentment — worry becomes their constant companion.

But those who live with *taqwa* — who guard their hearts from corruption and strive to remain God-fearing — they carry within them a peace unlike any other. It's the peace that comes from knowing their Lord is pleased with them.

Even such people face hardships — no life is free of them — but along with their trials comes a steadfast strength: **the strength of the Almighty Himself.**

For Mrs. Asia, this strength had become her greatest treasure. Every challenge, every uncertainty that came her way now met a calm heart and a steadfast trust in Allah's plan. She had learned that true peace is not the absence of trials but the quiet assurance that even in the darkest hour, one is never alone.

Time flowed quietly, carrying with it the seasons of change and growth. Years passed, and life unfolded for Mrs. Asia's children just as she had always prayed it would.

Hussain had completed his studies with remarkable dedication and was now working in a prestigious multinational company, holding a well-respected position that made his mother's heart swell with pride. His steady nature, humility, and quiet strength reminded everyone of his late father, Mr. Mustafa — a man whose values seemed to live on through his son.

Ayesha, on the other hand, had chosen a different path — one filled with ambition, challenge, and a touch of destiny. After completing her post-graduation, she set her sights on the UPSC examination, determined to join the civil services and serve her country. Her first attempt had taught her the value of discipline and strategy, and by the time she prepared for her second, she was sharper, more focused, and unshakably confident.

From the beginning, Ayesha had been clear with herself: she would give only two or three attempts, no more. If she didn't clear the exam, she had a plan B — to start her own business, something creative and independent. But Allah had written a different story for her.

Her second attempt turned out to be the turning point. She worked tirelessly for months — rising before dawn, revising through long nights, and practicing every mock test with fierce determination. Her room often echoed with the rustle of papers, the hum of concentration, and whispered prayers between chapters of thick books.

When the results were finally announced, Ayesha's name shone among the successful candidates. She had cleared the UPSC examination — one of the toughest in the country — in her second attempt. The moment felt surreal. For Mrs. Asia, it was as if all the struggles, tears, and quiet sacrifices of the past had found their meaning in that single triumph.

Within a few weeks, Ayesha received her posting as an IAS officer in a district. As she stood there on her first day of duty — dressed in her crisp formal attire, the badge glinting proudly on her chest — she felt a wave of gratitude wash over her.

It wasn't just her victory. It was the victory of every silent prayer her mother had whispered into the night, every hardship they had endured together, and every ounce of faith they had placed in the Almighty's plan. The careful planning of the parents, their unwavering attention to their children, and the children's hard work — all of it finally bore fruit. Ayesha's achievement of becoming an IAS officer became a matter of immense pride for the entire family.

For Mrs. Asia, it was not just her daughter's success, but a validation of her own strength, faith, and integrity. Her dignity, her determination, and her good deeds had not gone in vain. She had lived a respectable life under her own roof — never depending on any relative for favors, nor ever entertaining their unsolicited advice.

Over the years, many had tried to "advise" her — telling her not to give so much freedom to a girl without a father, to marry Ayesha off early, and to stop worrying about education or ambitions. But Mrs. Asia never paid attention to such voices. She did only what her late husband, Mr. Mustafa, would have done for their children had he been alive.

Her self-respect, her independence, her quiet insistence on making her own decisions — these things unsettled many in the extended family. Out of jealousy or resentment, they often spoke ill of her behind her back. They whispered that she was too proud, too modern, too distant from tradition. But time, as always, has its own way of revealing the truth.

Now, with Ayesha's name shining among the nation's civil servants, the same people who once criticized Mrs. Asia had changed their tune completely. Their tone had softened, their smiles had become warmer, and their words were dripping with admiration. Some even began to suggest matrimonial alliances — for their sons, of course.

Even Mrs. Zulaikha, who had once mocked and doubted her, came forward with a sense of entitlement, saying proudly, "Ayesha has always been like our own daughter. I've always wanted her to become our daughter-in-law. She belongs in our home."

But Ayesha had other plans. Marriage was not something she was ready for — not yet. She was determined, clear-headed, and deeply focused on her purpose. She wanted to devote herself to her work, to serve honestly and bring positive change to society. She dreamed of using her position, her authority, and her voice to stand up for justice and help those who could not help themselves.

Ayesha believed that power was not a privilege — it was a responsibility. She had grown up on the islamic values of truth, compassion, and courage. Her mother had raised her to never lie, never tolerate oppression, and never stay silent when witnessing injustice. These were not just teachings to her — they were part of her soul.

But when she stepped into the real world — the world of bureaucracy and politics — she discovered how difficult it was to live by those ideals. Every step seemed to demand a compromise of her faith, her ethics, her sense of right and wrong.

If a corrupt builder had constructed an illegal building, or if a local strongman had seized public land, Ayesha's conscience urged her to act. Yet her hands were tied — there were "orders from above." Ministers had instructed that no action was to be taken.

Each such moment felt like a battle between her duty and her faith — between what was right and what was allowed. The authority she had once dreamed of using for good now felt like a burden shackled by invisible chains. In fact, it was only after joining the department that Ayesha truly understood the *extent* of corruption that plagued the system. What she had once heard in passing — in news reports, in Bollywood movies— now unfolded before her eyes in its raw, unsettling reality.

Police officers, ministers, judges, MLAs — people entrusted with upholding justice and serving the nation — most of them seemed utterly shameless, indifferent, and corrupt. There were a few honest souls, yes, but they were like scattered stars in a sky clouded with greed.

In her first six months as an IAS officer, Ayesha had worked with extraordinary passion and sincerity. She poured her heart into every assignment, determined to make a difference, to live up to the oath she had taken. She stayed late in the office, spoke directly with villagers and workers, refused bribes, and insisted that things be done the right way — fairly, transparently, truthfully.

But soon, reality began to press in from all sides. Her integrity, instead of being a matter for admiration, became a problem — an inconvenience to those who had long learned to benefit from the system's rot. Files would mysteriously go missing, her orders would be delayed, and her superiors would warn her — subtly at first, then more openly — not to "interfere too much."

Day by day, Ayesha's spirit began to feel heavier. She had entered the service with dreams of reforming society, of being a voice for justice — but the very institution meant to uphold justice was steeped in corruption and dishonesty.

And though she still carried herself with dignity and courage, there were nights when she sat alone in her room, staring out at the dark hills beyond her window, wondering if honesty had any place left in a world so tangled in lies. It wasn't as if Ayesha had never met honest people in the department — she had, but they were few, not enough to make a mark or make their presence felt. Gradually, she began to understand that the ideals she had once cherished, the dreams that had inspired her to become an IAS officer, had little to do with the reality she now faced. The truth of the world outside was harsh, far harsher than she had ever imagined.

In her district there was a stretch of fertile land—ancestral, worked for generations, the only livelihood of families who had never wanted anything else from the world except to be left in peace with their fields. Powerful builders had identified it for a commercial project. What followed was the kind of negotiation that looks, on paper, like an agreement and feels, in reality, like a siege. The farmers were persuaded, or worn down, or manoeuvred — the exact mechanism hardly matters because the outcome is always the same. They signed. The builders moved in.

And then the farmers discovered they had not been paid in full.

They came to Ayesha's office — poor, tired, carrying documents they had been told to trust and which had betrayed them. They sat across from her desk and told her what had happened in the plain, unadorned language of people who do not have the luxury of euphemism. She listened to every word. She looked at their faces. She understood immediately, from the shape of the transaction and the names involved, that colleagues within the government machinery had been part of what was done to them.

She issued a legal notice. She ordered construction halted.

For almost two months, the project stood still. During those two months, the pressure arrived from every direction — superiors, builders, people she had thought of as professional allies whose masks she now watched slip with a certain grim clarity. An enormous bribe was placed before her, the kind of number that is designed to make a person recalculate their values. She refused it. Threats followed — specific, serious, the kind that are not empty. She did not move.

In the end they transferred her out of the district. It was tidier than anything confrontational and achieved the same result. Within days of her departure, construction resumed. The farmers, still unpaid, began their journey through the endless corridors of a system that had already decided not to hear them.

During her short tenure, Ayesha had seen the worst kind of atrocities — illegal land grabs, cases of missing girls, minor rape victims, and countless stories of exploitation.

She had done what she could for each of them. Honestly, carefully, with everything her position allowed. She had not looked away from a single file. She had not traded a single case for an easier life.

One day in her new office she saw some known faces. The farmers she had left behind came to meet her in her new office after her transfer. They were so accustomed to dealing with her that even if she had gone many hundred kilometres away, they came to take her counsel. Their eyes brimming with tears — something inside her broke.

For the first time in her life, Ayesha felt truly helpless. She had fought the system from within, but now she realized that sometimes, the system itself was the enemy. Exhausted from battling corruption on all sides, she made the boldest decision of her life.

That very day, after the farmers left her office, Ayesha wrote her resignation letter.

Ayesha's resignation became, overnight, a question that hung heavy over everyone who knew her — most painfully over her mother and the extended family. In their eyes it was an inexplicable act. At family gatherings, Ayesha was the centre of all the gossips. Some people said she had quit out of fear — that the pressure from powerful men and the threat of violence had finally frightened her into walking away. Others were crueller: they called her foolish, arguing that corruption is everywhere and that no sensible person abandons such a respectable post for the sake of impossible ideals. Conversations that began politely at the tea table soon slid into speculation; strangers in the neighbourhood made it sound as if Ayesha had committed a social faux pas rather than performed an act of conscience. Rumour shops opened, and people bartered the narrative they found most comforting.

None of these versions came close to the truth.

Ayesha's decision was neither the surrender of a frightened woman nor the impulsive gesture of someone swept away by emotion. It had been a choice made with precise thought and fierce moral clarity. She had become an IAS officer because she wanted to change things — to steer society toward fairness, to extend a hand to those whose dignity had been flattened by poverty and power. But she had learned, in the slow and bitter arithmetic of two years on the job, how circumscribed the possibility of change could be. For an honest Muslim woman committed to her principles, the daily calculus of governance was unforgiving: time and again she found herself squaring her integrity against a machine designed to grind it down. To remain honest in that world required a kind of continual self-compromise, a quiet surrender of small things that, added together, made up one's soul. The case of the farmers was only the most visible wound. There were other violences too — caste cruelties that smiled from bureaucratic reports, the racism threaded into casual directives, the gangsterism that softened into "local practice," and the terrible, humiliating cases of molestation and missing girls that landed on her desk like accusations the system itself refused to answer. She had opened files that smelled of sweat and blood and had read statements in which truth was both weapon and pleading. Sometimes, after midnight, she would sit alone in her flat and re-read the names of those she had tried to help, and a hollow fear would rise in her chest.

That fear was not the mortal dread other people imagined. It was a spiritual unease — khauf-e-khuda, the fear of God — a trembling about complicity. Ayesha worried less about being harmed than about being, however unwittingly, the instrument of harm. She feared that, by signing the papers, by allowing a meeting to proceed, by choosing the "practical" over the "just," she might end up lending the state's machinery to the very oppressors she had sworn to confront. She remembered specific moments that gnawed at her. The day she had to stamp a memo that would delay the farmers' remaining payments for another month; the afternoon she was told, in a voice that tried to sound helpful, that "process" meant patience even when patience meant starvation for a household. She recalled the night the bribe was offered and the polite smile that accompanied it, the way the suitcase of money seemed absurdly mundane — like a tool dropped casually on a workbench. She thought of the mothers who came to her office with children clinging to their skirts and the way those women's eyes went from pleading to accusing, not in anger, but in the strangest sadness, as if asking, "Is the world meant to be like this?"

Her resignation, then, was an act of refusal: a refusal to let the machinery of state rebrand her conscience as compliance.

Outside, the world continued to narrate its easier stories. People preferred simpler explanations to the discomfort of moral complexity. But in Ayesha's own lonely interior, the decision glittered with a different clarity. It was not dramatic in the way gossip made it sound; it was not heroic in any headline sense. It was an intimate covenant between a woman and her conscience — a quiet, and necessary thing.

It had been six months since Ayesha resigned. Half a year since she had folded away the crisp white files, returned her government ID, and walked out of the office where she had once believed she could change the world. The world, however, had changed her first.

In those six months, the silence around her had grown into something almost tangible. Her relatives often came to visit her mother, Mrs. Asia, and the conversation, without fail, would circle back to the same question: "So, what is Ayesha planning to do now?"

Mrs. Asia never had an answer that satisfied them. She would smile vaguely, stir the tea, and say something like, "She's thinking... she'll decide soon." But in truth, she didn't know. Ayesha didn't speak much about her plans — perhaps because she didn't have any, or perhaps because she was still searching for something that would make sense again.

At first, her phone had kept ringing. Friends from the service called out of concern, some out of curiosity. A few tried to console her, others wanted to argue — to convince her she had made a mistake. But after a while, Ayesha stopped taking their calls. She had begun to feel that every conversation with them tugged her back into a life she was trying to leave behind. They spoke the language of postings and promotions, of transfers and political pressure, of reforms and red tape — the language of a world she no longer belonged to.

Gradually, the distance between her and her old life widened until it felt like another existence altogether — something she had lived in a previous birth. Becoming an IAS officer, the pride, the struggle, the resignation — all of it had turned into an *old chapter* of her story, one she had no desire to reopen.

In truth, Ayesha had long moved past everything that once weighed her down. She had buried the noise of gossip, the sting of judgment, and the ache of disappointment beneath a quiet determination. Life had drawn her into a new kind of struggle — one that was gentler in pace, yet far deeper in purpose.

After resigning from the civil service, she joined an NGO in Delhi that worked to protect underprivileged children from the many cruelties of society — exploitation, neglect, and the everyday violence of poverty. The organization helped educate these children, rebuild their confidence, and guide them toward a future that might otherwise have been denied to them.

Thanks to her years in the IAS, Ayesha already possessed valuable experience, influence, and a network of contacts among the city's educated and well-placed families. Combined with her natural intelligence and unshakeable work ethic, these qualities quickly earned her a high position in the NGO. Within a few months, she was appointed as its Director.

And then, in just two years, she achieved yet another dream — one she had quietly nurtured for a long time: to become a businesswoman. She started an interior design company that grew with astonishing speed, expanding across the city and beyond. Her name, once associated with bureaucracy and government service, now appeared in lifestyle magazines and entrepreneurship panels.

Around the same time, Ayesha married. It was a simple ceremony — elegant and sincere, like her — and soon after, she found herself content in ways she hadn't imagined possible. Her personal life began to settle into a rhythm of calm companionship, laughter, and purpose.

From IAS officer to NGO Director to successful entrepreneur, the list of Ayesha's achievements seemed endless. But when she looked back, she realized that none of these titles defined her. What truly gave her peace was the sight of the children she worked with — their shy smiles, their newfound confidence, the spark of hope that lit their eyes when they learned something new. Each small transformation felt like a victory far greater than any bureaucratic award.

At the NGO, she was free. She made her own decisions, led her team with conviction, and acted on her conscience without fear or interference. For Ayesha, that freedom — the freedom to act with honesty and compassion — was more rewarding than any government position could ever be.

And as for the relatives, the critics, the trolls — they had been there yesterday, they were there today, and they would remain tomorrow. Their words no longer touched her. She had learned that some lives are not meant to be explained or justified; they are meant to be lived, fully and fearlessly.

Ayesha had found her peace — not in power, not in recognition, but in purpose.

Ayesha was the kind of woman who turned every intention into reality. Whatever she set her mind to, she made it happen. IAS officer, NGO director, businesswoman — each dream she had once whispered to herself had come to life, one after another. People often wondered: how could someone be so lucky?

But luck had very little to do with it. The real answer lay behind her believe in herself, which was developed through the strength of her upbringing, in the values instilled by her parents, and in the foresight with which they had built their children's future.

When her father, Mr. Mustafa, was alive, he had lived with a simple but profound principle: that his children should never have to depend on anyone, and that they should never be deprived of education, no matter what. He believed that true security didn't come from wealth or influence, but from the ability to stand on one's own feet. Mrs. Asia, his wife, shared that belief — and after his passing, she carried it forward with remarkable courage.

Raising two children alone was never easy, but Mrs. Asia did it with quiet dignity and fierce determination. While others might have bowed under the weight of widowhood and responsibility, she refused to let hardship define her children's destiny. She worked tirelessly, managing the home, the finances, and the emotional chaos that grief leaves behind — yet she did it all without bitterness.

Life, however, had not been kind to the family. Hussain and Ayesha had lost their father early — both of them still children when they became orphans. And as often happens in such stories, their relatives treated them with the kind of indifference and pity that the world usually reserves for the powerless. The help that should have come from family arrived late or not at all; the affection that was owed to them was replaced by polite distance.

But Ayesha and Hussain had something far more precious than sympathy — they had their mother. Mrs. Asia was not just a mother; she was a fortress. She taught them resilience not through sermons but through example. She taught them that dignity was not a luxury but a right. That hard work was the only inheritance that could not be stolen. That self-respect was worth more than any inheritance or name.

Mr. Mustafa's timely planning had ensured they had access to good schools and a stable foundation, but it was their mother's love and unwavering faith that taught them how to use that foundation to build a life. From her, they learned what it meant to work hard and to hold one's head high — to walk through the world neither as victims nor as beggars of sympathy, but as self-reliant, self-respecting individuals.

Ayesha's confidence, her independence, her radiant optimism — none of it was accidental. It was the legacy of two parents who, even in the face of loss, had given their children the greatest gift imaginable: the courage to live with honor, and the strength to never bow before life's trials.

* * * * *

Chapter 6

Fabiha – God Matters

Fabiha had always been the kind of child who made teachers pause.

Not because she was difficult or demanding, but because of the quality of her attention — the way she absorbed information, turned it over, asked the question that arrived three steps ahead of where the lesson currently was. From the time she was old enough to hold a pencil properly, she had been consistently, quietly, formidably excellent. Top of her class, year after year, with the kind of consistency that is not luck but character. Gold medals at national Olympiads. Recognition at the international level. A shelf of certificates that told, in the formal language of academic achievement, the story of a mind that simply would not stop working.

She lived in Saharanpur with her parents — her father, Mr. Jameel, a steady and contented man who worked at the district electricity department and asked nothing dramatic of life; her mother, Mrs. Aqsa, who ran the household with the focused competence of a woman for whom home was both occupation and vocation. They were a middle-class family in the truest sense — not wealthy, not struggling, but purposeful. Education mattered in this house. Respect mattered. Stability mattered. Fabiha was their only child, and their hopes had arranged themselves entirely around her.

Now she was preparing for her Class 12 board examinations, and the intensity of her focus had reached a level that occasionally alarmed the people around her. She barely emerged from her room. Meals were consumed without particular attention to what was being eaten. Sleep was negotiated rather than enjoyed. She had targets, she had a plan, and she was the kind of person who, having made a plan, executes it with a completeness that leaves very little room for anything else.

The future she was working toward was specific and vivid in her mind: computer science engineering, a reputed college in Delhi, a hostel room that was entirely her own, and then a career in technology built by her own hands and her own intelligence. She had held this vision for years — not as a vague aspiration but as a destination with a route already mapped.

The difficulty was that not everyone in her life was reading the same map.

Fabiha's extended family — maternal and paternal, most of them scattered across the same city — gathered frequently, as close families in Indian cities do. Weddings, festivals, birthdays, the casual Sunday afternoon visit that becomes a three-hour affair before anyone has quite decided it would. These gatherings were a regular texture of her life, warm and familiar and, increasingly, a source of a particular kind of exhaustion.

In her maternal family especially, there was a tradition so embedded it had become invisible to the people inside it: girls married young. Twenty, twenty-one — ideally while still studying, before the window narrowed. This was not presented as a limitation. It was presented as wisdom, as care, as the natural and correct ordering of a woman's life. The conversation about proposals needed to start early — two or three years of searching, after all, was the minimum — so the calculations began practically the moment a girl crossed into her teens.

Education, in this framework, was not without value. But its value was instrumental rather than intrinsic. It made a girl more marriageable, more accomplished in the eyes of prospective in-laws. It was a credential to be presented alongside good character and domestic capability, not a path toward independence or professional ambition. The idea of a career — a real one, chosen and pursued for its own sake — did not fit easily into this picture. Most of the girls Fabiha had grown up around had absorbed this framework so thoroughly they had stopped noticing it. Their dreams, if they had ever been large, had been quietly renegotiated downward without anyone naming the negotiation.

Fabiha had not renegotiated. Which made her, in the eyes of certain relatives, a situation that required addressing.

She's seventeen now. Said casually, over tea, as though the number itself contained a warning. *If you don't start looking soon, the good proposals will pass. Two or three years minimum to find the right match — you don't want to leave it too late.* The words were delivered warmly, with the genuine care of people who believed what they were saying, which made them harder to dismiss than outright hostility would have been.

Fabiha sat through these conversations and felt the specific frustration of a person watching their future be discussed as though they are not in the room. As though the plans she had made for herself — the engineering degree, the Delhi college, the career — were a charming but ultimately impractical detour from the route everyone had already agreed she would take.

Mrs. Aqsa loved her daughter. This was not in question.

But love, filtered through a lifetime of absorbed beliefs, does not always take the shape the beloved needs it to take. Mrs. Aqsa had grown up in a world where a woman's competence was measured by her domestic capability, and she carried this measuring stick into her motherhood with the best of intentions. *You're seventeen — when you get married, will you bring shame upon us if you don't know how to cook?* She meant it as guidance. Fabiha heard it as a verdict on where her life was already assumed to be heading.

Mr. Jameel was different. Quieter about it, but different — the kind of father who watches his daughter receive a gold medal and feels a pride that does not immediately calculate its matrimonial value.

It was Mr. Jameel who eventually stood firm on the matter of Bangalore.

Fabiha had been selected, in Class 10, for a state-level competition — a significant achievement, the kind that arrives as confirmation of everything her teachers had been saying about her for years. The school was sending three students to Bangalore, accompanied by teachers. It was the opportunity exactly as Fabiha had always imagined opportunities — real, specific, earned.

Mrs. Aqsa would not hear of it.

The world was unsafe. Society had become dangerous. Girls could not be sent alone, could not be trusted to environments their mothers had not personally inspected, could not — *could not* — be allowed to travel that far without a family member present. These fears were not invented; they came from a real place. But they had calcified, over years of repetition, into a wall rather than a concern — a wall that stood between Fabiha and every open door that appeared in her path.

If Fabiha had been a son, there would have been no wall. Mrs. Aqsa would not have needed a single conversation to decide. She would have packed his bag.

It took Mr. Jameel's patient persistence and a personal appeal from the school principal before Mrs. Aqsa finally, reluctantly, agreed.

Fabiha went to Bangalore.

She came back with the first prize trophy.

When the three students walked into the school with the trophy, their parents were already waiting in the courtyard, and the happiness in that gathering was the uncomplicated kind — parents and teachers and children all united in the simple pleasure of a thing going exactly as it should. The teachers could not stop talking about how Fabiha and her teammates had conducted themselves — the discipline, the confidence, the quality of their work under pressure.

Mr. Jameel stood listening to all of this with the quiet radiance of a father who has believed in his daughter for years and is watching the rest of the world catch up.

Mrs. Aqsa smiled too. In that moment, at least, the pride was uncomplicated.

The trophy was still in Fabiha's hands when her mother ended the excitement.

They were in the car, heading home, and Fabiha was talking — properly talking, the way she rarely got to talk, with all the excitement of someone who has just lived through something significant and wants to share every detail of it before the feeling fades. The competition, the other schools, the moment they announced the result, the look on her teammates' faces — she was mid-sentence, animated and happy, when Mrs. Aqsa interrupted.

"That's enough. This was the first and last time we allowed you to go somewhere like this. From now on, no competitions that require traveling to another city."

The car continued moving. Outside, Saharanpur passed by in the early evening light. Inside, Fabiha went quiet.

She looked down at the trophy in her hands — the thing she had worked for, traveled for, competed for and won — and felt it become, in the space of a single sentence, insufficient. Not enough to change anything. Not enough to shift the story her mother had already written for her. The excitement that had been filling her chest since the result was announced drained away with a speed that was almost physical.

Mr. Jameel had been watching.

"Stop." His voice was firm in the way that quiet men's voices become firm when they have reached a limit. *"Our daughter has just come home after winning. And this is what you say to her?"*

Mrs. Aqsa said nothing more. But the damage, as Fabiha understood, had already been done — not by this one remark, but by the remark's confirmation of everything she already suspected. That no achievement would be large enough to move her mother's priorities. That the life being planned for her would continue to be planned regardless of what she accomplished or wanted or demonstrated she was capable of.

Mr. Jameel understood this too. And he made a decision.

He told Fabiha, quietly and without theatre, that he would take her wherever she needed to go. Competitions, college visits, examinations in other cities — wherever her ambitions required her to be, he would be there. She would not have to fight that particular battle alone.

Something settled in Fabiha when he said this. Not the resolution of everything — her mother's views had not changed, the extended family's expectations had not changed, the cultural current she was swimming against had not changed. But she was no longer swimming entirely alone. Her father's promise was a fixed point she could orient herself by, and for a girl whose inner life had become increasingly isolated, a fixed point was everything.

Her room became her world.

Not in the sad, contracted sense of someone who has retreated from life, but in the focused, purposeful sense of someone who has decided exactly what she is working toward and has organised everything else accordingly. Books, notes, a desk that knew the shape of her elbows by now, and dreams that she had stopped apologising for and simply pursued. Computer science engineering. Delhi. A college that would take her seriously. A future built on what she was actually capable of, not on what was traditionally expected of girls in her family.

Alongside her technical studies, Fabiha read widely — history, civilisation, the lives of people who had built something from nothing or changed the direction of their fields through sheer refusal to accept the limits others placed on them. She watched interviews, studied how exceptional people thought, understood that achievement at the highest level was never accidental. This intellectual curiosity set her apart from her cousins in ways that were occasionally lonely but never, to her mind, regrettable.

Most of the girls she had grown up around had, by seventeen or eighteen, shifted their primary attention toward clothes, jewellery, appearance — not because they were shallow, but because they had been raised in an environment that consistently told them these were the things that mattered for the future being prepared for them. Marriage proposals were already being discussed. Families were already calculating timelines. The girls had absorbed the framework they had been handed and shaped their ambitions accordingly, which is what people do when no one shows them an alternative.

Fabiha had been shown an alternative. She intended to take it.

But the gap between her and her mother continued to widen in ways that cost her more than she showed.

Mrs. Aqsa was not a cruel woman. She was a woman shaped by her own upbringing, carrying forward the beliefs she had been given by her mother, who had carried forward the beliefs given to her, and so on — a chain of inherited assumptions about what a girl's life should look like, each link forged with genuine love and equally genuine limitation. She wanted good things for Fabiha. She simply had a very specific and traditional idea of what good things meant.

Higher education in another city was not among them. The money it would cost — money Mrs. Aqsa had been mentally allocating toward dowry, toward the furniture and gold and household items that would accompany her daughter into her marriage — felt to her like a misdirection of resources. Fabiha's academic excellence was something she was proud of, in the way you are proud of a quality that enhances your child's prospects. It was not something she read as a signpost pointing toward a particular kind of independent future.

This meant that Fabiha navigated her most demanding years — the pressure of Class 12, the competitive examinations, the sustained intensity of preparing for a future that required her to be consistently exceptional — largely without her mother's emotional support. She did not talk to Mrs. Aqsa about the anxiety that had begun to settle into her days, the restlessness and irritability and emotional sensitivity that she could feel but could not quite name. There was no point. The conversations they had about her future moved in circles that always returned to the same place.

What Mrs. Aqsa did not see, because Fabiha did not show her, was the cost of all this. The toll of carrying ambition in an environment that treats it as a problem to be managed rather than a quality to be nurtured. The feeling of loneliness in the world where nobody in your immediate family shares the idea of future which you believe in.

Mr. Jameel saw it. And he stayed true to his promise — the forms, the examination registrations, the practical support that made the abstract dream into a series of concrete steps. He showed up, quietly and consistently, for all of it.

Fabiha showed up for the rest.

When the Class 12 results came, she had scored 98.7%.

The anxiety-filled months of preparation, the pressure she had carried largely alone, the determination she had maintained in the face of a home environment that was, at best, ambivalent about what she was working toward — all of it had resolved into this number. She read it and felt something that was not quite triumph and not quite relief but something that lived between the two: the particular satisfaction of a person who set an enormous goal for themselves and did not flinch from the work it required.

She had also secured admission to a good engineering college in Delhi.

The dream had, against a fair amount of resistance, remained intact.

Then the campaign began.

It was not organised, exactly — it never is in families. It was simply the natural result of people who share a set of beliefs encountering a situation that challenges them and responding with the tools they have always used. Conversations. Repeated concerns. The patient, persistent application of social pressure to a point of resistance until the point gives way.

The point, this time, was Mr. Jameel.

"Jameel, will you really send your daughter alone to Delhi? The environment there is very bad. Fabiha is such a simple, innocent girl — the world is clever and cruel. What will you do if something goes wrong?"

It was said by one person and then another and then several more, each repetition adding a little more weight to the pile they were building on top of his daughter's future. They meant it. That was the thing that made it difficult — they were not manufacturing fear for strategic reasons. They genuinely believed what they were saying. They had simply never examined where those beliefs came from, or whether they were being applied fairly, or whether the same concerns would have been raised if the child going to Delhi for an engineering degree had been a son.

They would not have been. Everyone in the room knew this, though no one said it aloud.

Mr. Jameel listened to all of it. He had always been a patient man.

He was also a man who had watched his daughter return from Bangalore with a first prize trophy and had heard her go quiet in the back seat of a car on the drive home. He had made her a promise. He had no intention of breaking it.

Mr. Jameel did not argue with the relatives. He did not explain himself, did not justify his decision, did not engage with the parade of concerns that were presented to him over tea and across dinner tables with the confident authority of people who have never had to examine their own assumptions.

He simply knew his daughter.

He knew her capabilities and her discipline and the quality of her determination — had watched it operate, up close, for seventeen years. The relatives saw a girl. Mr. Jameel saw a person with a specific and serious future ahead of her, and he understood that his job was to make sure the road was clear enough for her to reach it. Everything else was noise.

When Fabiha's admission to the Delhi engineering college was confirmed, he turned his attention immediately to the next practical problem: where she would live. He approached this with the same methodical care he brought to everything that concerned his daughter. Fifteen PG accommodations visited in person. Each one inspected — the facilities, the security arrangements, the neighbourhood, the other residents, the management, the feel of the place at different times of day. He was not looking for somewhere adequate. He was looking for somewhere he could leave his daughter and drive back to Saharanpur without the particular anxiety of a father who is not sure he has done enough.

He found it. He made sure of everything. And then, a few days later, Fabiha moved in.

The first weeks in Delhi were something she had no previous experience to measure against.

A new city, a new college, a room that was entirely her own, decisions made without anyone's permission or commentary — for a girl who had spent her entire life negotiating the space between her own ambitions and her family's expectations, this tasted like something she did not yet have a word for. Freedom was part of it. But it was more specific than that. It was the freedom of being taken seriously — by the city, by the college, by the daily requirement of managing her own life. She was not a girl to be worried about or married off or cautioned against taking up too much space. She was an engineering student in Delhi, and the world, for once, was treating her accordingly.

The phone calls home developed a distinct pattern.

With her father: long, warm, detailed — the kind of conversation between two people who actually want to know how the other is doing. With her mother: brief. A greeting exchanged, a confirmation that she was eating and sleeping adequately, and then the call ended before it could become something more complicated. Fabiha had not decided to create this distance. It had simply grown, naturally, out of years of conversations that had not given her what she needed, and the understanding — quiet but certain — that Mrs. Aqsa's vision of her daughter's life and her own vision of it were oriented in fundamentally different directions.

She had been in Delhi a little over a month when the hostel began to show its less appealing dimensions.

The petty thefts were the most exhausting thing — not because of what was taken, but because of what they represented. Food from the shared refrigerator, prepared carefully the evening before and gone by morning. Clothes that disappeared from the laundry area and reappeared, later, on someone else. These were small violations, each one individually manageable and collectively maddening. The girls who did it were the same girls who greeted her pleasantly in the corridor, who appeared in class taking notes with focused expressions, who presented, in every visible way, the face of educated and reasonable people.

Fabiha found this genuinely difficult to reconcile.

Her friends in the hostel offered the obvious solution: reciprocate. If people take your things, take theirs. Everyone does it. It evens out. This was presented as practical wisdom, the natural adaptation of a person who has understood how the environment works and adjusted accordingly.

Fabiha listened to this advice and did not take it. Not out of naivety — she understood exactly what was being suggested and why. But she had a question she kept returning to: if she became the kind of person who takes what does not belong to her, what exactly has she preserved in coming all this way? Her marks? Her degree? Those things mattered. But they were not the whole of what she was trying to build. Her values were not a set of rules imposed from outside. They were the actual substance of who she was. Compromising them for convenience — even small, reasonable-sounding convenience — was a trade she was not willing to make.

So she absorbed the thefts and held her ground and paid the price of it in minor, recurring frustration.

One evening, she came home from college hollowed out by the kind of exhaustion that is not just physical — the accumulated weight of a long day, hostel politics, the low-grade stress of living in an environment that required constant vigilance. She did her laundry. She went to the kitchen. The food she had prepared for herself that morning was gone.

She went to her room and sat on her bed and cried.

Not dramatically. Not with any particular resolution to stop. She was simply tired, and hungry, and far from home, and the combination of those things had reached the threshold that even the most determined person eventually reaches.

She called her mother.

She was not calling to complain — she understood this about herself even in the moment. She was calling because she needed the specific comfort of a mother's voice, needed to be heard without judgment, needed someone to say *I know it's hard, but you're doing well, and I'm proud of you.* She had earned that, many times over.

Mrs. Aqsa listened to what she was saying.

Then she said: *"It was your own choice to live in a hostel and stay on your own. Now you must face the consequences yourself."*

Fabiha held the phone for a moment after that. Then she set it down.

She sat in her room in Delhi, in the PG her father had spent days finding for her, in the city she had fought to be allowed to come to, and understood — not for the first time, but more completely than before — that she was not going to receive from her mother the thing she kept hoping to receive. This was not anger, exactly. It was a sadder and more final kind of knowledge. The kind you stop arguing with.

She did not call back that evening.

The first year of college was, by any honest accounting, difficult.

The environment around her was one she had not been prepared for by anything in her previous experience. Girls smoked in the common areas without self-consciousness. Alcohol was a routine social currency, consumed openly and without the furtiveness that Fabiha might have expected. Live-in relationships were not whispered about — they were simply part of the landscape, as ordinary and unremarkable as any other feature of college life. None of this was presented as transgression. It was simply how things were here, and if you found it surprising, that was your problem to adjust to.

Fabiha watched all of it and felt, in turns, bewildered and entirely clear.

Bewildered because the distance between this world and the one she had grown up in was larger than she had anticipated. Clear because none of it tempted her, even slightly. She was not holding herself back from these things through effort or willpower. She simply had no desire for them. Her values were not a cage she was straining against — they were the ground she stood on, and she stood on them comfortably. The girls around her were making their choices. She was making hers.

She studied. She focused. She showed up for every class with the same quality of attention she had brought to every exam since she was old enough to hold a pencil.

At the end of the first year, Fabiha topped her batch.

She read her results and felt the quiet, specific satisfaction of a person who has been told repeatedly — by circumstance, by environment, by a mother who said *face the consequences yourself* — that the path they have chosen is too hard, and who has chosen it anyway, and who has been proven right.

It was not the last time she would need to prove it. But it was, for now, enough.

The second year brought Nancy.

She arrived at the hostel the way certain people arrive in any shared space — loudly, with an immediate and destabilising effect on the atmosphere. Dominant, argumentative, perpetually in conflict with someone. In a private hostel where girls came and went with the regularity of seasons, she was simply the latest addition to the rotation. Nobody knew much about her — her real name, where she was from, what she was actually studying or whether she was studying at all. Nobody particularly needed to know. Everyone was busy with their own lives, their own pressures, their own carefully maintained distance from other people's drama.

What nobody had accounted for was Nancy's specific fixation on Fabiha.

It began as jealousy, which is common enough in close quarters — the low-grade resentment that can develop when someone else's qualities feel, somehow, like a comment on your own. Fabiha's intelligence bothered Nancy. Her looks bothered Nancy. But what bothered her most, in a way that seemed almost personal, was Fabiha's modesty — the way she dressed, the way she moved through the world without performing herself for anyone's approval. It was so different from Nancy's own presentation that it seemed to function, in Nancy's mind, as a silent criticism. Which it was not. But jealousy rarely requires accuracy.

The sarcasm started first. Comments delivered within earshot, designed to land without being directly confrontational. Taunts in the common area, timed for maximum audience. Nancy was skilled at this — at the particular art of humiliation that maintains plausible deniability, that can be laughed off as a joke if challenged. Fabiha absorbed these without response. Not because she was afraid of Nancy, but because she had looked at the situation clearly and calculated that engagement was a waste of resources she needed for better things. Her first year results were in. Her teachers thought highly of her. She was thinking about postgraduate study in the United States. Nancy was simply not a priority.

This indifference, predictably, made things worse.

In a hostel of ninety-five girls, Fabiha had become, without particularly trying, someone people liked. She did not take what wasn't hers. She helped when asked. She kept her drama — of which she had none — entirely to herself. Her reputation was the natural consequence of her character, accumulated over months of small, consistent choices. Nancy, by contrast, had cultivated the opposite reputation through the opposite choices, and the contrast was not flattering to her.

Fabiha had become, in Nancy's eyes, intolerable.

The escalation was gradual and then suddenly not gradual at all. Cigarette burns appeared in Fabiha's clothes — small, deliberate, precisely placed where they would ruin the garment. Her phone number was distributed to strangers. Messages arrived — obscene, unsolicited, from numbers she did not recognise — and the fear that came with them was the specific fear of a woman who understands she is being watched without knowing by whom or from where.

Then came the phone call.

Fabiha had come out of the bathroom, hair still wet, and sat in the common area with a book. An unknown number called. A boy's voice said, calmly and with the particular satisfaction of someone delivering a message they have been given: "*You look very beautiful in a red suit with wet hair.*"

She went still.

The book was still in her hands. The common area was still around her. Everything continued as it had been a moment before, and yet something had changed in the quality of the air. She was being watched. She did not know from where or by whom, but the information in that sentence — the colour of her clothes, the wetness of her hair, the exact moment she had sat down — left no room for another interpretation.

In the corner of her vision, Nancy was watching. Enjoying, in the specific way of people who cause suffering and find it satisfying, the fear on Fabiha's face.

Fabiha said nothing to anyone.

Not to her mother — she already knew what that conversation would produce. Not to her father — she loved him too much to place this on him from a distance, and she feared, with the particular fear of a child who has watched a parent worry, what it might do to him. She carried it alone, which is what she had learned to do with most things, and she kept going to class and kept studying and kept building toward the future that she was not going to allow Nancy or fear or anything else to take from her.

But the fear lived in her now, low and constant, the way a sound you cannot locate lives in a room.

She noticed other things too, in those weeks. A change in the way people looked at her — or didn't look at her. Conversations that stopped when she entered. Girls who had previously been friendly now offered her glances she couldn't quite read: part pity, part something more complicated, part the deliberate avoidance of someone who has seen something they don't know how to address.

She asked directly, because that was her nature. *What's going on? Why does everyone start whispering when I walk past?*

She received sarcastic looks in return. A mocking comment. The turned back of someone who had decided not to be involved.

Fabiha did not yet know what had been done to her.

Nancy had obtained photographs — taken at a hostel event, innocent and public, the kind of pictures that exist in any shared living situation. She had used them. With the help of AI tools that had made this particular cruelty newly available to anyone with a grievance and a smart phone, she had created images and videos that had nothing to do with Fabiha except her face — images designed to humiliate, to destroy, to take the thing a person has built of their reputation and reduce it to something they would not recognise.

She had uploaded them on social media. They had been circulating for ten to fifteen days.

Fabiha had been the last to know, because she was not much on social media, because she had been too busy studying to notice the weather changing around her, because nothing in her experience had prepared her for the possibility that someone could do this — could reach into the privacy of her face and weaponise it.

She was twenty years old, two hundred kilometres from home, and she was about to find out.

The warden's summons came on an ordinary afternoon.

Fabiha had known, in the way you know things before you can name them, that something was wrong. The shifted glances, the conversations that stopped, the roommate who had gone silent without explanation — she had been reading these signs for days without being able to decode them. Now, walking toward the warden's office with her heart already braced for something, she still could not have prepared for what was waiting inside.

The warden looked at her with an expression Fabiha had never seen directed at her before — not disappointment exactly, but something colder. The particular look of a person who believes they have been deceived.

"I always thought you were a decent and respectable girl," she said. *"But you turned out to be completely immoral."*

The ground did not literally move. But something in Fabiha's body registered it as though it had.

The warden showed her the images. The videos.

Fabiha looked at them and understood, in one terrible moment, what had been done to her — and how long it had been circulating while she studied and attended class and moved through her days in complete ignorance. Her face. Her face, used for something she had never done, had never imagined, had never in her life been remotely close to. Weaponised and distributed to the people who knew her, to the people who had respected her, to the warden who was now looking at her as though she were someone else entirely.

She broke.

"Ma'am, please — please believe me. This is not me. I haven't done this. These are fake."

She was crying before she had finished the sentence — not the controlled, manageable tears of someone who has decided to show emotion, but the helpless, total crying of a person whose world has just collapsed beneath them without warning. She was pleading, which was something Fabiha had never done before in her life, because she had never before needed to plead for belief in her own character.

Outside the office, the hostel girls had gathered. Word travels fast in close quarters, and this had been travelling for days. They stood and watched. And Nancy stood among them, performing concern with the practiced ease of someone who has engineered the very disaster they are now commenting on. *"I always thought she was so decent,"* she said, to no one in particular and everyone within earshot. *"But look at what she turned out to be."*

The warden told Fabiha she could no longer stay. Her parents had already been contacted.

They arrived while she was still packing.

She walked into the warden's office carrying her luggage and saw her parents sitting there, and the sight of them — her father's face, her mother's — broke something else open in her chest. She had not been able to stop crying since the warden's office, and she could not stop now.

Before she could say a word, Mrs. Aqsa stood up and slapped her across the face.

The room went very quiet.

Fabiha stood where she was. She did not raise her hand to her cheek. She did not speak. She absorbed it in the way she had absorbed many things — in silence, holding herself as still as possible, while inside something that had been holding on very hard finally let go.

The warden asked Mr. Jameel to sign the register. They left.

The journey from Delhi to Saharanpur was two hundred kilometres of her mother's voice.

Mrs. Aqsa did not stop. The words came in waves — accusations, recriminations, the bitter satisfaction of a woman who had warned against exactly this and been overruled and was now watching her worst fears apparently confirmed. *This is why I was against sending girls away. She has left us with no face to show the family. She has crossed all limits.*

In the front seat, Mr. Jameel drove and said nothing. His silence was its own kind of weight — not the silence of a man who had nothing to say, but the silence of a man who could not trust his voice, who was holding himself together with great effort and very little left to work with.

Mrs. Aqsa pulled Fabiha's hair. She hit her again.

Fabiha tried, again and again, to say the words that felt like the only true things left in her world: *the pictures are fake. The videos are not mine. Please believe me. Please.* The words came out small and exhausted, stripped of the conviction they deserved because she had already said them so many times to so many people who had looked through her rather than at her.

Nobody believed her.

She had not eaten since morning. The day had been too full of things that were not food.

That night, in her room in Saharanpur, Fabiha lay down and did not get up. The scenes played on a loop behind her eyes — the warden's face, the crowd of girls outside the office, Nancy's performance of concern, the slap in the silent room, her mother's voice for two hundred kilometres. Her dignity. The thing she had guarded so carefully, through all the hostel politics and the stolen food and the threatening phone calls and the obscene messages — the thing she had considered non-negotiable, the thing she had refused to trade for anything — had been taken from her without her knowledge or consent, by someone who had decided, for reasons rooted in nothing more than jealousy, that she deserved to be destroyed.

She could not look at the images again. She would not. But she could not stop seeing them either.

At some point in the night, she lost consciousness.

Mrs. Aqsa came in to give her something to eat and found her lying still, and the fear that moved through her in that moment — the specific, primal fear of a mother confronting the possibility of the worst — was immediate and total. She screamed for Mr. Jameel.

He came running. They both bent over their daughter — checking her breathing, speaking her name, the frantic tenderness of parents who have, in the space of a single day, gone from signing a hostel register to this. They brought her back. They gave her water. She opened her eyes.

The fever came soon after.

Through the night, Fabiha drifted in and out — and in those drifting moments, she kept saying the same thing, over and over, in the small broken voice of someone who is no longer fully conscious but is still, underneath everything, trying to be believed:

"Papa. I haven't done anything. Please believe me. The videos are fake."

Mr. Jameel sat beside his daughter and wept. He had believed her from the first moment. He had believed her in the warden's office and on the road and now in this room, and the believing of it — the full understanding of what had been done to her and by whom and how completely — was more than he could hold without it showing.

"I know, my child," he kept telling her, each time she surfaced enough to hear him. *"I know you did nothing wrong."*

The next morning he took leave from work and did not leave the house.

When the fever had come down slightly, he asked Mrs. Aqsa to take Fabiha her breakfast. He said it carefully: *"Take it to her. And please — say nothing negative."*

Mrs. Aqsa carried the tray into Fabiha's room.

Fabiha, sitting in her bed, flinched when her mother entered. It was involuntary — the body's honest response to an association it had formed over the past day, between her mother's presence and pain.

Mrs. Aqsa placed the tray on the bedside table. She said: *"Have your breakfast."* Then she left.

No question. No hand on her daughter's forehead. No acknowledgment of the magnitude of what Fabiha was living through. Just the tray, placed and departed, in the silence of a mother who did not know — or could not bring herself — to offer what her daughter most needed.

Fabiha looked at the food and did not touch it.

She understood something now that she had been approaching for a long time from a distance and had finally arrived at fully: that the crisis she was in had two parts. The external one — Nancy, the images, the hostel, the warden — was real and devastating. But the internal one, the one happening inside the four walls of her own home, was in some ways worse. Because Nancy was a stranger whose cruelty was legible and external. Her mother was the person who was supposed to be the fixed point when everything else came loose. And the fixed point was not holding.

The breakfast tray sat untouched. Outside, the morning continued with its ordinary business.

Inside Fabiha, something that had been bending under enormous pressure for a very long time finally bent far enough to be called by its proper name.

Depression settled in. Quietly, completely, the way serious things settle when they have been kept waiting long enough.

Fabiha did not know for sure whether Nancy was behind it.

She knew only the damage — the images, the warden's face, her mother's hand across her cheek, the two hundred kilometres of accusations, the breakfast tray placed in silence and taken away untouched. She lay in her room in Saharanpur and built, from these materials, an understanding of the world that depression does what depression always does: it took the most painful interpretation available and made it feel like the only true one.

Nancy had destroyed her reputation. But her mother had not believed her. And somehow, in the arithmetic of Fabiha's broken state, the second betrayal had become larger than the first. Nancy was an enemy she had not chosen and had not seen coming. Her mother was supposed to be the one person whose belief required no proof, whose love was not conditional on the verdict of a hostel warden or the content of a social media post. The girl who had always loved her mother quietly, who had absorbed years of unreturned emotional support without letting the resentment show, now found that the thing she had been holding back had arrived all at once, and it was too large to contain.

She could not be in the same room as Mrs. Aqsa. Could not hear her voice without something inside her going rigid. Could not look at her without seeing the warden's office and the slap and the two hundred kilometres of words that had landed on her like stones while she sat there trying to say *please believe me, please, the images are not real.*

Relatives began to visit, as relatives do when something has gone wrong in a family and they want to understand it firsthand. Mr. Jameel and Mrs. Aqsa told everyone the images were fake. The relatives nodded and went home and continued to whisper, because that is what people do with stories like this. The damage was done and could not be undone by the truth, which arrives too late and too quietly to compete with scandal.

Fabiha sank. Mr. Jameel noticed the changes in her personality. As a responsible father he arranged therapy sessions for her.

Therapy helped, in the way that therapy helps when the wound is deep — not by closing it quickly, but by making it possible to remain functional while it heals slowly. She would feel lighter for a few days after each session. Then the weight would return, and she would feel it more than before, because the contrast had shown her how heavy it actually was.

Mr. Jameel watched his daughter and did everything a father could do from inside his own helplessness. One day, he sat near her bed. He asked, gently, when she thought she might be ready to return to her studies.

Fabiha had no answer. The question felt like it was being asked in a language she no longer spoke.

Then Mrs. Zehra came home.

She was Mr. Jameel's elder sister, returned from the United States after three years away — a woman of considerable presence, the kind of person whose arrival changes the air in a house. She was wise and warm and deeply faithful and had never in her life confused the comfortable thing with the right thing. She adored Fabiha with the specific devotion of an aunt who has recognised something exceptional in a child and made it her business to say so, loudly and often, in a family that did not always say it enough.

She had known what was happening. She had been in contact with Mr. Jameel throughout, asking about Fabiha with the focused concern of someone who is not asking out of politeness. She arrived knowing the shape of what she was walking into.

Fabiha who used to run to the door when her aunt arrived — who would embrace her before she had properly crossed the threshold, who would immediately begin telling her everything that had happened in the three years since she'd last seen her — did not come out of her room.

Mrs. Zehra set her luggage down. She sat for tea and the brief ceremony of arrival. And then she said, calmly, to Mrs. Aqsa: *"Call Fabiha. I'd like to see her."*

Mrs. Aqsa shifted. *"Let it be for now. These days she doesn't react well when I go to her room. I don't know how she'll be."*

Something moved across Mrs. Zehra's face — not anger exactly, but the expression of a person who has just had a suspicion confirmed.

"Aqsa," she said, quietly but with a weight that made the words land precisely, *"you have been deeply unjust to Fabiha."*

She walked away leaving Mrs. Aqsa sitting at the table, trying to understand what had just happened.

That evening at dinner, they were all at the table when Fabiha came in.

She sat down without looking at anyone. She began to eat in the focused, mechanical way of someone who is fuelling a body they are not currently inhabiting.

Mrs. Zehra looked at her across the table. *"How are you, my child?"* Her voice was warm — the specific warmth of someone who genuinely wants to know.

Fabiha said nothing. She kept her eyes on her plate.

Mrs. Aqsa, sitting beside her, did not waste time to shout on her. *"Did you not hear what your aunt asked you?"* She turned to Mrs. Zehra with the expression of a woman presenting evidence. *"You see for yourself — after bringing all this trouble on us, after shaming this entire family, she has become rude to everyone. Completely shameless."*

The table went quiet.

Mrs. Zehra's face changed. It was a visible change — the warmth that had been there a moment before replaced by something older and more authoritative.

"She has not brought trouble on anyone," she said. *"You are responsible for the troubles in her life."*

She stood up. She looked at her brother. *"Jameel. Come to my room. I need to speak with you."*

She walked out. The dinner continued without her, in the particular silence of a table where something has just been said that cannot be taken back.

Later, after Isha, Mrs. Zehra came to Fabiha's door.

She knocked gently. *"May I come in, my dear?"*

"Aunt." Fabiha's voice came from inside, careful and contained. *"Please don't come in right now. I don't feel like talking to anyone."*

"Just five minutes," Mrs. Zehra said. Not a demand. An offering.

A pause. Long enough that it might have been a refusal.

Then: *"Alright. You can come in."*

Mrs. Zehra entered quietly. She had brought things from America — Fabiha's favourite chocolates, and a white jacket that Fabiha had mentioned wanting, once, in a different version of her life when wanting things had still felt possible. She placed them in her hands without ceremony.

Fabiha thanked her. Briefly, formally, her emotions held carefully behind her eyes.

Mrs. Zehra turned to leave. She reached the doorway and stopped.

"Fabiha, my child," she said, without turning around. *"I came here for you. Only for you. To stand beside you, to find a way through this together. I'm not going anywhere until things are better. Whenever you need to talk — whenever you're ready — I'll be right next door."*

She stepped out into the corridor.

For a moment, nothing happened.

Then Fabiha moved.

And the next moment she ran and wrapped her hands around her aunt and started crying. And she was crying in the way she had not been able to cry since everything began — not the helpless, terrified crying of the warden's office, not the silent crying of the car journey, but the crying of someone who has finally, after a very long time, found a place that is safe enough to fall apart in.

Mrs. Zehra held her and said nothing for a while. Just held her.

Then she said, softly, into Fabiha's hair: *"Now it truly feels like I've come to India. Because my Fabiha ran to me herself."*

In Fabiha's family, most of the conversations were meaning less gossips: who wore what, who spent how much, whose daughter had married well, whose son-in-law had disappointed. The currency of these gatherings was appearance — how things looked from the outside, how the family was positioned in the eyes of other families, whether the gold was good and the clothes were expensive and the match was respectable.

Fabiha had never been able to make herself care about any of it. Not out of arrogance — she was not an arrogant person — but because the conversations felt like standing in a shallow pool when she knew the ocean existed. She kept her distance from cousins her own age and was quietly labelled for it: *proud*, they said. *Thinks she's better than everyone.*

She was not proud. She was simply elsewhere in her mind, most of the time, and could not manufacture enthusiasm for discussions that felt like they were about the surface of things rather than the substance.

Mrs. Zehra understood this completely, because she was the same.

When they were together — and they had been together, over the years, and those were the cherished memories of Fabiha — they talked about history, about science, about books and films and ideas that had weight. They argued about things worth arguing about. They laughed at things that were genuinely funny. Mrs. Zehra saw in her niece a mind that deserved to be taken seriously, and she took it seriously, and this was so different from Fabiha's usual experience of being seen that it felt, every time, like water after a long thirst.

Mrs. Zehra had no daughters. Perhaps that was part of it. She had looked at Fabiha and seen something she recognised and loved, and she had never once made her feel like a future bride to be packaged and delivered. She had made her feel like a person.

"I wish she were my own," she used to say to Mrs. Aqsa, about Fabiha. *"You are truly fortunate."*

Mrs. Aqsa would smile and say nothing much, because she could not quite see what Mrs. Zehra was seeing, and did not know that Fabiha was listening, and did not know what those words meant to a girl who was searching, constantly and quietly, for evidence that her own mother was proud of her.

That night, holding Mrs. Zehra in the doorway of her room, Fabiha cried until the first acute wave had passed. Then Mrs. Zehra sat her down and said, gently: *"You've cried enough, my child. Now tell me everything — slowly, calmly. And then we'll think together about what to do."*

Fabiha told her.

All of it — the messages from unknown numbers, Nancy and her methods, the phone call about the red suit and the wet hair, the images the warden had shown her, the crowd of girls outside the office watching, the slap in the silent room, the two hundred kilometres of her mother's voice, the breakfast tray placed without a word and taken away untouched. She spoke until she had emptied herself of it, and the tears ran continuously through the telling, and Mrs. Zehra sat beside her and listened with the full, undivided attention of someone who has come specifically to hear this and is not going to look away from any part of it.

And then, at the end of it, Fabiha said the thing she had been holding at the very bottom of herself.

"Aunt — I feel like disappearing from this world. I don't want anyone to know me. I don't want to talk to anyone." Her voice had gone quiet and very dull. *"I want to die, Phuppo. I want to die."*

The words landed in the room and changed it.

Mrs. Zehra did not flinch. She did not immediately redirect or reassure or try to talk Fabiha away from what she had just said. She held her, and she let the words exist, and she understood them for what they were: not a plan, but a measure of pain. The expression of a person who has been carrying more than a person should have to carry, alone, for longer than anyone should have to carry it, and who has run out of ways to say *I cannot do this anymore* except this one.

The screaming that followed brought Mrs. Aqsa to the door.

The moment Fabiha saw her mother, something broke open further. The words came from a place beyond composure

— raw and unfiltered and true in the way that only things said in extremis are true.

"Since the day I was born I have only been a source of trouble for you. Why do you always see me as the problem?"

"My own mother doesn't trust me. My achievements don't make her happy. Wanting to be an engineer was my mistake. And now, when someone has wronged me, when false videos have been spread about me — you still say it's my fault."

Mrs. Zehra turned to Mrs. Aqsa. Her voice was quiet but absolutely clear: *"Please go outside."*

Mrs. Aqsa did not move. She was frozen in the way of a person confronting something they had not expected and cannot immediately process.

"Aqsa. Go."

And Fabiha, through her tears: *"Please leave. Stay away from me."*

Mrs. Aqsa left. The door closed. Mrs. Zehra stayed.

Later, when Fabiha had finally exhausted herself and stilled, Mrs. Zehra came out of the room and found Mrs. Aqsa on the sofa. She was crying — and there was genuine distress in it, the distress of a mother who has just heard her child say she wants to die and cannot reach her, cannot be the person who helps, because she is the wound rather than the medicine.

"Did you see?" Mrs. Aqsa said, through tears. *"She holds me responsible for everything. I'm already so distressed — relatives, neighbours, everyone has distanced themselves from us. I was only being strict so that we wouldn't have to face days like this."*

Mrs. Zehra looked at her sister-in-law for a long moment.

Then she said: *"Enough. Be quiet."*

It was not unkind. But it was not gentle either. It was the voice of a woman who has run out of patience for a particular kind of self-involvement at a moment that requires something else entirely.

"What kind of mother are you?" she said. *"Your daughter has just told you she wants to leave this world. And you are sitting here talking about neighbours? About your reputation?"*

"Allah gave you an exalted position — the position of a mother. He gave you an intelligent, obedient, virtuous daughter, and in her most broken hour you are not standing beside her. You are thinking about yourself. Your loss. Your name in the family."

Mrs. Aqsa opened her mouth.

"You should have been her rock," Mrs. Zehra continued. *"You should have believed her without needing proof. A mother's belief is not supposed to be conditional."*

She paused, and when she spoke again her voice was quieter but no less clear.

"What happened to Fabiha was not your fault. The girl who did this to her — that is not on you. But everything Fabiha cried out about you tonight? Every word of it was true."

"You never acknowledged her achievements. When she brought home medals, you received them as though they were ordinary. That girl spent years watching your face for one sign — just one — that you were proud of her. You never gave her that sign."

"And the greatest injustice," Mrs. Zehra said, her voice dropping to something almost sorrowful, *"is that you never helped her build a relationship with Allah. You never taught her prayer as a discipline, never showed her faith as a foundation, never gave her the trust in Him that would have held her when everything else fell away. You left her spiritually empty, Aqsa. And when the storm came, she had nothing to hold onto."*

The room was very quiet.

Mrs. Aqsa sat with what had just been said, and the tears continued, and for the first time in a long time, they were not entirely about herself.

Mrs. Zehra paused at the doorway of her room and said it simply, without drama, as though it were already decided: *"For a few days, I'm taking Fabiha to our ancestral home. God willing, things will begin to improve."*

The next morning, she sat with her brother and was equally direct.

"All the videos, the photographs, the links — everything needs to be reported to cybercrime authorities. This should have been done weeks ago."

Mr. Jameel had known this. But Mrs. Aqsa's fears had been louder than his own instincts — the fear that involving the police would compound the shame, that going to the authorities would make the story more public rather than less, that silence was the safer shelter. He had listened to those fears and waited, and the waiting had cost Fabiha weeks of additional suffering while the images remained online and Nancy remained untouched.

Watching his sister now — her clarity, her refusal to be managed by fear — something shifted in Mr. Jameel. He had been a good father in most of the ways that counted. In this one, he had been too patient, too deferential to his wife's anxiety. He would not be anymore.

Mrs. Zehra's husband and in-laws were influential people who moved within elite social circles that included senior police officers and ministers. She used these connections with the careful deliberateness of someone who understands that influence is a tool and tools should be used precisely.

Over two or three days of quiet, continuous work — calls, conversations, the patient navigation of systems that respond to the right pressure applied in the right places — a proper investigation was initiated. Social media accounts, links, the digital trail that Nancy had left behind in her cruelty: all of it was being followed, systematically and with the kind of attention that produces results.

On another front, Mrs. Zehra packed a bag for Fabiha and took her away.

The ancestral haveli existed in a different register of time.

It was old in the way that certain buildings are old — not neglected, but seasoned, carrying in its walls and courtyards and high-ceilinged rooms the accumulated weight of generations who had lived fully within them. Mrs. Zehra had grown up here. She had dreamed here for the first time, studied here, become herself here in the slow and unhurried way that is only possible in places where no one is rushing you toward a destination. She took the responsibility of Haveli's maintenance and used to send money from across the world for its upkeep, as though keeping it intact was a form of keeping faith with her own past.

The garden held mango trees and guava and pomegranate, and a small vegetable plot tended by the household staff with the quiet pride of people who understand what it means to grow things. The verandah ran long and wide with four arch-shaped doorways that gave the whole space an old-world elegance — and in it, among the things that had survived undisturbed across decades, stood an old wooden swing that had belonged to Mrs. Zehra's grandfather, still sturdy, still graceful, as though time had decided to leave it alone out of respect.

Beside it: two large wooden prayer platforms, placed side by side.

When they arrived, the cook had anticipated them — chicken qorma, mutton biryani, shahi toast for afters. The July heat that pressed on the rest of the city did not seem to reach inside the haveli, which breathed with the cool indifference of thick old walls and high ceilings. The smell of the food moved through the corridors to meet them at the door.

Mrs. Zehra rested and freshened up. Then she and Fabiha sat together at the dining table and ate.

Fabiha ate. Slowly, without much appetite, but she ate. And Mrs. Zehra, watching her, noticed something she had not seen in days: the slightest easing of the tension that had taken up permanent residence in Fabiha's face. The haveli was already doing something. Quietly, without announcement, the way healing always begins — not with a grand gesture but with a slight loosening of the thing that has been held too tight.

"My child," Mrs. Zehra said, when the meal was done, *"I want to see you return to life. So for just a few days, trust me and do as I say. Think of it as a small request from your aunt."*

Fabiha looked at her and nodded. One small nod. It was enough.

"Bano," Mrs. Zehra called to the maid, *"place both prayer platforms together in the verandah."* She turned to Fabiha. *"After lunch, make your ablution. We'll pray together."*

She set an alarm on her phone for each of the five prayers. Then she picked up Fabiha's phone and set the same alarms on it. *"When the alarm rings,"* she said simply, *"we meet at the platforms."*

The first two days were effortful.

Fabiha was not accustomed to the structure of it — the ablution before each prayer, the five fixed points in the day that required her presence regardless of what else was happening, the discipline of meeting a commitment that did not negotiate with her mood or her exhaustion. It felt unfamiliar in the way that anything feels unfamiliar when you have not been given it as a child and are encountering it properly for the first time as an adult. She came each time because she had promised, and a promise to Mrs. Zehra was not something she would break. But she came out of duty rather than desire, out of love for her aunt rather than any particular feeling about the prayer itself.

By the third day, something had shifted slightly.

By the fourth, she noticed she was looking forward to it.

There was something in the bowing, in the prostration — the physical act of placing your forehead on the ground, of making yourself small before something infinitely large — that did something to the tightness she had been carrying for months. She could not have explained it in technical terms. She only knew that when she rose from prayer she felt, briefly and consistently, something she had almost forgotten was available to her: peace. Not the peace which she attained because of the change of her setting, but a different kind — the peace of a person who has just been reminded that they are not alone in the universe, that there is a Presence that has been listening all along.

She was surprised by this. She had not expected it.

The days took on a shape.

Mornings: prayers, then the garden — Fabiha's hands in the soil, the small satisfying work of tending things that grow. Afternoons: the kitchen, where Mrs. Zehra cooked herself together with Fabiha. Fabiha enjoyed it very much, trying things, making mistakes, laughing occasionally at the mistakes, which was something she had not done in a long time. Evenings: tea on the verandah, and then, before Maghrib, Mrs. Zehra would open a short passage of the Qur'an and they would sit with it together.

Not in the formal way of a lesson. In the way of two people thinking through something together, turning it over, asking what it means and why it was said and what it offers to a person reading it now, in this life, with these specific circumstances.

The Qur'an, Mrs. Zehra had always believed, is not a text you read at a distance. It is a world you enter. And once you are inside it, it begins to work on you in ways that are not always immediately visible but are nonetheless real.

She asked Fabiha one evening: *why do you think Allah tells us the story of Prophet Yusuf in such detail? Why do we need to know that the cruelty came from his own brothers — from the people who were supposed to love him? Why do we need to know about the well, the years of wrongful imprisonment, the long patience before the turning?*

Fabiha sat with the question.

And why Prophet Ayub — why the account of his suffering, specific and prolonged and given to us in the Qur'an not to be explained away but to be witnessed? What is Allah saying to the person who reads these stories in the middle of their own darkness?

The verandah was quiet around them. The old swing moved slightly in the evening air. The pomegranate tree stood in the garden with its particular stillness.

Fabiha did not have a complete answer yet. But she was beginning, for the first time in months, to ask the questions. And asking the questions was itself a return — to curiosity, to engagement, to the part of herself that had always believed the world was worth understanding.

Mrs. Zehra watched her niece's face in the fading evening light and felt something settle in her own chest.

The spark was still there. Dimmed, buried under everything that had been done to her and everything that had been withheld from her — but present. Undestroyed.

She would nurture it back. That was why she had come.

The answers to big questions rarely arrive all at once.

They come in increments — a word that lands differently than it did before, a moment of stillness in which something previously obscured becomes briefly visible, a realisation that arrives not as a thunderclap but as a quiet settling, like sediment finding the bottom of still water. This is how Fabiha's journey began: not with a dramatic turning point, but with small, daily accumulations of something she had never been given enough of before.

At twenty-one, Fabiha had never been particularly consistent in her prayers. She had read the Qur'an before—yes—but she had never truly understood it. Now, little by little, something within her was changing. Gradually, she began to emerge from the shadows of her trauma. A connection with Allah was forming—soft at first, then stronger with each passing day. The prayer mats spread out in the veranda now felt like the safest place in the world, and lowering her head in sujood felt like the most profound peace she had ever known.

What had happened to her in the hostel had not vanished from her memory. She still remembered it clearly. But it no longer shattered her every day. It no longer consumed her or made her physically ill. Mrs. Zehra's plan was working. Fabiha was healing—without counseling, without medication. The Qur'an itself was becoming her remedy.

One morning, after the Fajr prayer, Mrs. Zehra and Fabiha sat side by side in the veranda. Dark, heavy clouds were gathering rapidly in the sky, and the air carried a soothing stillness—the kind that comes just before a downpour. The weather was beautiful, almost comforting. Bano, Mrs. Zehra's house help, served them breakfast right there: hot aloo parathas and freshly prepared sandwiches, still warm from the pan.

Fabiha looked genuinely happy—calm and content. She laughed and joked with Mrs. Zehra just as she used to before the incident, and seeing this filled Mrs. Zehra's heart with quiet joy. Watching Fabiha return, slowly but surely, to herself was a relief beyond words. Her condition was improving, and it was finally clear—Fabiha was healing.

Mrs. Zehra was quite happy with the way Fabiha was recuperating, but she could not forget the words of Fabiha which she uttered when she was in pain.

"Aunt — I feel like disappearing from this world. I don't want anyone to know me. I don't want to talk to anyone. I want to die, Phuppo. I want to die."

Those words still send a chill up her spine. So, one morning she sat down with Fabiha and started talking about Surah Maryam.

Not with a lecture or a lesson — with a story, told the way Mrs. Zehra told all the things worth telling — slowly, with attention to the details that matter, with the understanding that a story lands differently when you are not rushing toward its conclusion.

She spoke of Maryam's devotion, her purity, the quality of her worship that was so evident and so consistent that Prophet Zakariyah marvelled at it and asked Allah for a child of similar righteousness. She spoke of the honour Allah placed on Maryam — an entire chapter of the Qur'an bearing her name, the only woman given this distinction in all of scripture.

And then she spoke of the trial.

"When Isa was born," Mrs. Zehra said, her voice quietening, *"the cruelest attack was not on her body. It was on her dignity."*

The people who had respected Maryam — who had spoken of her piety, who had held her in high esteem — began to whisper. The admiration was replaced by accusation. The trust was replaced by doubt. She who had been the most known for her purity was now the most doubted among her people.

And she had faced this alone. In the hardship of childbirth, without a comforting hand, without a reassuring voice. The physical pain and the dread of what awaited her when she faced her community. In that moment of deep sorrow and helplessness, a cry escaped her heart — a wish to be spared from witnessing the humiliation she feared would follow.

Mrs. Zehra paused.

The verandah was very quiet. The clouds had come closer. Somewhere in the garden, a bird was making a sound it would stop making when the rain arrived.

"That was only a phase," Mrs. Zehra said. *"A moment in her life. A passage through the darkest point before the light."*

Because Allah had chosen Maryam for something that no accusation could undo — to be the mother of Prophet Isa PBUH, to be honoured in His book for every generation until the end of time. Her dignity had not been destroyed by what people said about her. It had been preserved, permanently and completely, by what Allah wrote about her.

Fabiha listened. She had been listening with her whole body, in the way she listened to things that were finding something in her rather than merely entering her ears. The story was not abstract. It was not history. It felt as if the story was speaking directly to her wounds.

Her eyes filled.

the tears came — quietly at first, then steadily, flowing without restraint.

And then, underneath the grief, something else arrived.

A clarity.

It does not matter what people think of you. What matters is what Allah knows about you.

And with that realization came a deep and long lasting peace.

The thought that Allah knew her truth, that in His sight she was pure and innocent, filled her heart with comfort. A new strength stirred within her, steady and warm. The fear and the shame that once haunted her began to fade, as though they had been quietly lifted from her shoulders.

She made a promise to herself, there in the rain-smell and the silence. She would live for one purpose: to seek Allah's consent. Whatever her mother could or could not understand, whatever the relatives said, whatever the world decided about her based on images that had nothing to do with who she actually was — she would hold what was right and keep moving. With dignity. Without bitterness.

She had found, somewhere inside herself, a ground that was hers and could not be taken.

With the realization that they were all servants of Allah, and that life's trials were only part of the journey, she found a new sense of direction. Obstacles would come, hardships would appear, but she would remain on the path she now believed in.

After a long moment, she turned to Mrs. Zehra.

"I want to go back," she said. Her voice was quiet but it had something in it that had not been there before — a steadiness, a direction. *"I want to return to college. I've already lost so much time. I don't want to lose any more."*

Mrs. Zehra looked at her niece.

The pride in her eyes was the kind that does not need to announce itself. The relief was the kind that comes only after a real fear has been genuinely resolved. She opened her mouth to speak — to tell Fabiha how far she had come, how strong she was, how proud she had made her. But before she could speak, her phone rang.

Mr. Jameel's voice came through with the particular quality of a man who has been carrying something heavy and has just been allowed to put it down. The cyber police had solved the case. The digital trail — the accounts, the links, the AI-generated images — had been followed to its source. Nancy had been arrested from the hostel.

Mrs. Zehra listened. Then she lowered the phone and turned to Fabiha and told her everything.

Fabiha sat very still for a moment.

Around them, the rain that had been threatening all morning finally arrived — soft at first, then steady, falling on the mango trees and the pomegranate and the old wooden swing, filling the verandah with the smell of wet earth and the sound of water finding its way through leaves. It was, without anyone planning it, exactly the right weather for this moment.

The gap had closed. The truth, which had existed all along, had been confirmed in the language the world requires — evidence, investigation, arrest — and the person who had weaponised her face against her was being held accountable.

Two days later, Mrs. Zehra was leaving for the United States. On the same day, Fabiha was leaving for Delhi.

They stood at the door of the haveli — the haveli with its courtyard and its garden and its prayer platforms and the verandah where so much had been slowly, quietly repaired — and Fabiha held her aunt and did not immediately let go.

"Phuppo," she said, her voice muffled against Mrs. Zehra's shoulder, *"we'll meet again soon."*

Mrs. Zehra kissed her forehead. Her eyes were full. *"My brave child,"* she said. *"Allah Hafiz. And don't ever stop praying."*

It was a simple goodbye. It contained everything.

Walking back into college required a particular kind of courage that is different from the courage required to face external threats.

The corridors were the same. The classrooms were the same. The professors, the canteen worker, the students who had once whispered when she walked past — all of them were the same. But they had formed opinions about her, and opinions, once formed, do not dissolve simply because the truth has been established elsewhere. She would have to walk through their lingering judgments every day, with her head up, and keep going.

She was no longer afraid. This surprised her, a little. She had expected to be.

Mr. Jameel came with her. He sat with the Head of Department and explained everything — calmly, completely, without embellishment. The Head of Department was the kind of person who listens before he concludes, and he listened carefully. Then he called in several professors and spoke in Fabiha's favour openly and without reservation. He acknowledged what she had endured. He acknowledged her courage in returning.

And then he asked if she would be willing to speak to the students.

Not to narrate her suffering as spectacle, but to give them something useful: an understanding of how these things happen, how to protect themselves, how to recognise manipulation and cruelty in the digital spaces they all inhabited. Young women living in hostels, navigating independence for the first time, needed to hear this from someone who had lived it and survived it and come back.

Fabiha stood before the students and spoke.

She was not the Fabiha who had arrived in Delhi two years ago — eager and slightly overwhelmed and entirely unprepared for what was coming. She was not the Fabiha who had sat on the floor of the warden's office crying *please believe me, please.* She was someone who had passed through those versions of herself and come out the other side knowing things that cannot be learned any other way.

The students listened. Some of them recognised themselves in what she described. Some of them understood, for the first time, the specific vulnerability of a good reputation in the hands of someone who has decided to target it. All of them saw, in the woman standing before them, something worth paying attention to.

The whispers faded. They were replaced by something else — a respect that had the particular quality of being earned through difficulty rather than simply granted. Fabiha made more friends in her remaining years at college than she had in the first. Professors pointed to her in conversations about resilience. Students came to her when they needed someone who would tell them the truth.

She completed her engineering degree with the dedication of someone who understands, in full, what the opportunity cost.

Engineering Degree followed by another feather in Fabiha's crown, she got admission in one of the prestigious universities in USA. The dream she had held quietly since childhood — the one that had survived her mother's resistance and Nancy's cruelty and a depression that had once made her want to disappear from the world entirely — had not been extinguished. It had simply been waiting.

Back in Saharanpur, Mrs. Aqsa had changed.

Not dramatically, not all at once — people rarely change that way. She no longer spoke of marriage as the primary measure of Fabiha's worth. She watched her daughter from a distance — the engineering degree, the postgraduate admission abroad, the speech that had changed the atmosphere of an entire college — and felt something she had not always known how to feel toward Fabiha: straightforward, uncomplicated pride.

Underneath it, quieter and more private, was the regret. The knowledge that the role she should have played — the believing, the encouraging, the teaching of faith as something real and sustaining rather than merely nominal — had been played instead by Zehra Phuppo. She was grateful for this. She was also honest enough with herself to know what it meant.

In the United States, Fabiha met Zubair.

He was her classmate — American-born, the product of a family that had carried their faith and their values across an ocean and raised their son inside them. He was thoughtful and principled and his conversation had the quality of someone who had read widely and thought carefully and arrived at his beliefs through genuine engagement rather than inheritance. They talked about ideas. They found, to both their quiet surprise, that they were largely looking at the world through the same glasses.

What began as academic discussion became, gradually, mutual recognition. And then, over time, something more.

When the conversation moved toward marriage, Mrs. Aqsa advised Fabiha to leave the past where it was. The cyber police had removed everything. There was no trace online. Nobody needed to know. It would have been the easy thing, the practical thing, the thing most people would have chosen without a second thought.

Fabiha listened to her mother. Then she listened to herself.

She had done nothing wrong. She carried no guilt, no shame. She was not the author of what had happened to her. She was its survivor.

And if she built a marriage on omission — on the careful management of a truth she had spent months learning to stand inside — what kind of foundation would that be? What kind of beginning?

She told him everything.

She did not narrate it as scandal or confession. She spoke of it the way she had come to understand it — as a trial, a passage, a chapter that had cost her greatly and given her, in return, a clarity about herself and her faith that she would not trade for anything. She spoke with the dignity of a person who knows exactly who she is and has decided that this knowledge is worth more than anyone's comfortable ignorance.

Zubair listened.

When she finished, he was quiet for a moment. Not the uncomfortable quiet of someone recalibrating their opinion. The quiet of someone who has just been given something precious and is taking a moment to understand its value.

His respect for her did not diminish. It deepened, in the way that respect deepens when you discover that the person you admire is even more admirable than you had realised. He had hoped to marry a woman of courage and faith and integrity — a woman who could walk through the world without being diminished by it, who could raise children with both the fear of Allah and the confidence to stand in their own dignity.

They married. The celebration was warm and genuine and full of people who loved them, and they stood together in it with the happiness of two people who have arrived at each other honestly, without pretence, without the management of inconvenient truths.

Mrs. Aqsa's long-held dream had been fulfilled. Her daughter was married into a good family, respected and loved. But the fulfilment looked nothing like she had imagined it when Fabiha was seventeen and she was cataloguing dowry items and worrying about proposals. It had come through a route she had not planned or approved of — through education and independence and a crisis that had nearly broken everything — and it was better, more solid, more real, than anything she had imagined.

She watched her daughter on her wedding day and felt the full complicated mixture of a mother who loves her child and knows she has not always shown it the right way and is grateful, beyond expression, that the child turned out so well despite that.

Fabiha had once sat in a room in Delhi and wished she could disappear from the world.

She stood now in a life she had built with her own hands, her own faith, her own honesty.

She had not arrived here by accident, or luck, or the absence of difficulty. She had her pie of hardships, for after every hardship there is relief. But in the process, she found her faith, the real meaning of her life.

* * * * *

www.ingramcontent.com/pod-product-compliance
Ingram Content Group UK Ltd.
Pitfield, Milton Keynes, MK11 3LW, UK
UKHW040038200726
13845UKWH00054B/490

9 789358 967692